MASONIC HALLS OF ENGLAND

The North

Opposite: *Whitby*.

MASONIC HALLS OF ENGLAND

THE NORTH

The Revd Neville Barker Cryer

LEWIS MASONIC
IAN ALLAN GROUP

In the same series

Masonic Halls of England—The Midlands

Masonic Halls of England—The South

Published by Lewis Masonic
IAN ALLAN REGALIA LTD, Terminal House, Shepperton
who are members of the
IAN ALLAN GROUP

First published in England in 1989

British Library Cataloguing in Publication Data

Cryer, Neville B.
Masonic halls of England.
The North.
1. England. Freemasons. Lodgers. Halls
I. Title
942

ISBN 0 85318 165 9

Printed in Great Britain by
Latimer Trend & Company Ltd, Plymouth

CONTENTS

FOREWORD

For more than a century Masonic historians have been concerned in researching the origins and development of the Craft. Little, however, appears to have been done in recording the most publicly visible evidence of our existence: the places where we meet. From my own experience of visiting lodges in England and Wales I know the great wealth of history and variation in style evidenced by the many Halls and Lodge Rooms used by our lodges. The Rev. Neville Barker Cryer is to be congratulated both for bringing this aspect of our history to our attention and for recording it now for those who will follow us in years to come.

M. B. S. Higham
Commander, R.N.
Grand Secretary.

PREFACE

THE WRITING OF this book, like the other volumes in this series, has given the author a great deal of pleasure. It has permitted me to appreciate something of the breadth and depth of English Freemasonry at the present time as well as allowing me the delight of seeing the wealth of treasures which we still possess and of meeting some of the dedicated masons who have undertaken to preserve for the future those heirlooms they have received from the past.

It has been a journey of constant surprises as door after door has been opened to reveal the temple interiors and their contents, sometimes in almost the same manner as they were first seen 150 or 100 years ago. It is the joy of that discovery, and the interest aroused in seeing so many items of peculiar fascination for the masonic student that led me to believe that we should produce this and the other volumes.

My first concern therefore has been to record for the present generation and for posterity something of what the Craft has handed down to us from its very beginnings in this land. Many, I believe will, like myself, be pleasantly surprised by the variety and richness of the different halls which are illustrated here, whether it be the sense of antiquity at Hull or York, the majestic hall and rooms of Manchester, the converted chapel at Beverley or the astonishing façade at Halifax. Every location has its own fascination especially when, as I hope I have shown, the building also contains particular treasures that are known nowhere else or only rarely so. I hope that this survey of intriguing Northern halls will raise the spirits of masons at this time and make them quietly proud of the heritage that is theirs.

The second purpose of my writing has been to try and encourage a greater diligence throughout our land in looking at and understanding the possessions in Freemasonry that we may have in our own locality. It has been my experience that my visit to a temple or its museum has often renewed interest in its contents for the masons who regularly and normally meet there. Too many of us are not aware of the treasure trove that lies around us and there is all the more danger that if this unconscious indifference is not stemmed there could be examples of the kind of loss of previous pieces of the past such as have already occurred in some centres and not least at Halifax. If you ask some masons in a place that has a long tradition where are their old tracing boards, chapter banners, globes or pillars the answer is either 'we don't know' or 'Ah! now we do have some stacked somewhere'. Once the items are unearthed and explained, there is a new sense of pride awakened and a determination to look after these heirlooms with more care.

Thirdly, I wanted to encourage masons who travel around the country to go and see some of the halls and their contents that are mentioned here. It has long been a custom for people on their holidays to enter an old parish church, a castle or manor house and wonder at the relics of the past of our nation. Here, for freemasons, is the beginning of a guide for some of our peculiar heritage in English history. I hope sincerely that readers will take this book with them on their journeys and ring up the local Provincial or lodge secretary and ask whether a visit to these halls is possible. It will well repay you to see these halls for yourself.

As I have travelled around this land and responded to the information about interesting halls that has been provided for me I have been only too well aware that

I may be overlooking some gems of masonic interest that I ought to have included here. Despite the fact that there will be at least two other volumes in the series with this one—covering the South of England and the Midlands—I am sure that there will be some who will want to draw my attention to treasures overlooked. With the encouragement of the publisher I invite anyone who would wish to do so to write to me at Shepperton and give me details of their hall and its contents. I am sure that future editions of this volume or others in the series can benefit from being kept as comprehensive as possible. It may even be that we shall find ourselves with enough material for yet another volume in the series. It will be good to know that this book has stimulated such interest in *Masonic Halls of England.*

The Revd Neville Barker Cryer
1988

ACKNOWLEDGEMENTS

NO BOOK SUCH as this could possibly have been completed without the help of a large number of collaborators. I shall attempt to name many of these below but it would be impossible to mention the countless Provincial Grand Masters, Provincial Secretaries and their staffs who have assisted me with suggestions, contacts, directions for travel, and in some cases actual hospitality. I am deeply grateful to them all and I want to state here that had it not been for them and their work then this book would not even have been possible, and certainly not in the time available.

Having been put in touch with individual halls, and the lodges associated with them, I specially want to thank the following for their interest before, during and following my visits and for being willing in each case to check the script of my chapter for their hall so that it is as accurate as possible. Any remaining errors must still be laid at my door.

(Alnwick) G. Miller; (Barton upon Humber) L. W. Cox, H. Cocking; (Berwick on Tweed) G. Dickson; (Beverley) L. Los; (Bolton) G. Battey; (Bradford) D. A. C. Herridge; (Durham) V. Ferens; (Huddersfield) F. Broadbent, N. Hirst; (Kingston upon Hull) C. G. Hopley; (Newcastle upon Tyne) G. A. Luckham; (Sunderland) R. W. Gibson, J. W. Heslop; (Wakefield) W. Read; (Warrrington) H. Boscow; (Whitby) K. Bull; (Whitehaven) E. Hall; (York) G. C. F. Halliwell. Thanks are also due to John Hamill, Librarian and Curator of the United Grand Lodge of England Library and Museum for assisting in the supply of illustrations. To numerous photographers who have supplied illustrations, some anonymously, and to all of these brethren, as well as many others whose names I have not recalled, I extend the very warmest of thanks and express my delight at making so many more masonic friends.

1 Alnwick
2 Barton Upon Humber
3 Berwick
4 Beverley
5 Bolton
6 Bradford
7 Carlisle
8 Durham
9 Huddersfield
10 Kingston upon Hull
11 Liverpool
12 Manchester
13 Newcastle Upon Tyne
14 Sunderland
15 Wakefield
16 Warrington
17 Whitby
18 Whitehaven
19 York
20 Halifax

ALNWICK

A Treasure House of Northumbria

THE VISITOR TO Alnwick in Northumberland will be tempted to seek out many places of interest in this ancient town. He may be drawn to the imposing presence of the great Castle of the Percy family, a bastion of England against the invader for most of a thousand years, but he can also be attracted by the well-preserved town square and its buildings and the northern gate with the Parish Church nearby.

Amongst the buildings to the west of the town, and yet in one of its oldest remaining quarters, is an ivy-covered hall that juts out into Prudhoe Street. Without windows, a shop 'The Old Bakery' on one side of it and a small, tree-covered and shrub-lined garden on the other it may not attract the attention of the passer-by, and yet here, in this quiet corner of northern England, we have a gem of a masonic hall, all the more precious because it is normally so unobtrusive and undisturbed. The building that now houses Alnwick Lodge No 1167 has been the local masonic home for over a century. Previously it was the Sunday School of the nearby St Paul's Church and its happy purchase in 1881 reveals that at least in those days the established church had no qualms about Freemasons using church property.

Yet the Masonry which came to reside in this present hall had had a long and chequered past. The visitor ought to know something of the heritage that he will here find traces of.

Prior to 1680 an Operative lodge kept records which continued to exist until 1919 when the widow of the last man to hold them burnt them, not realising their unique value! There are minute books, however, for 1701 to 1757, 1779 to 1824, and from 1867 to the present day, and in the opening pages of the first minute book is one of the last half-dozen copies extant of the old *Masons' Constitutions*, otherwise only known in the printed version found in Hughan's *Old Charges of British Freemasons* of which, naturally, this well-kept hall also has a copy.

From this first and the second volume (after 1779) it is worth noting the very heavy fines to be incurred for absence, swearing or 'calling another by any name but Fellow'; the gaps at the period of the Jacobite Rebellion; meeting at private houses and necessarily on 24 June and 27 December (the St John's days); the requirement in 1748 that 'None shall be admitted to the said lodge under the age of 21 *or above 40*'; the names of two members actually involved in rebuilding Alnwick Castle; all contributing to a Sword (cost 6s) 'excepting Paul Renwick who is dead'; a procession to church in 1784 where the Rev Bro Fisher was to preach the sermon; and the resignation of Bro Dent, owner of the 'Beehive', meaning that the lodge moved to Bro Daglish's 'Turk's Head'.

Some idea of the local speech is also retained in the mention that the 'Comote meat tomorry (Committee meet tomorrow) to take remarks of the reason why sartain members have absented themselves for several months past', whilst an impression of the 'brotherly love' expressed locally is shown by the despatch to Morpeth in 1791 of 'Five Silver Ornaments, Six sashes, Colours, two Colour staffs, Hammer, two pillars'. Next year it was obviously recognised that there was need of attention to the lodge's own possessions for 'the Truncheons, Mallet and Rods be painted and a crimson satin cushion be made and bound with gold binding'.

In 1797 there was a visiting brother from St David's, Berwick (see elsewhere in this volume) and in 1804 the return to the Clerk of the Peace shows that there were 58 members including a Hatter, Mariner, Excise Man, Chemist, a Miller, Musician, Servant in Regt of Scots Greys, Painter (who is to paint to the value of his Initiation money!), Engineer, Carpenter, Blacksmith, Butcher, Millwright, Tobacconist, Sergeant-Major, Gamekeeper and Gentleman. Further seeking for a home led to a petition in 1820 to ask Earl Percy, Duke of Northumberland, to fit up the Hotspur Tower in the Castle as a lodge room. It seems not to have been

Looking west showing the impressive sideboard upon which is placed the tripod and perfect ashlar. The two unusual pillars can also been seen in this view.

granted for in 1824 the lodge closed for a time since three members were not paying dues and 'too high Initiation Fees prevented many respectable persons from joining', and in 1867, when the lodge was reopened, it was held at the Freemasons' Hall, Freemasons' Tavern in the Market Place. The brotherly love continues for in 1874 the Almoner assists six Scotch, two English, one German, one Cape Town and one Isle of Man Masons with 3s each!

The Earl Percy, who was now the Provincial Grand Master, entertained the Province (about 700 persons) at the Castle in 1878 and hence served 44 gallons of soup, 22 Turbots and the same dishes of eels, 66 dishes of Venison, 132 Roast and 66 Boiled Fowls, vast numbers of pies and 84 Jellies with the same number of Pastry dishes, etc, etc 'to the greatest satisfaction of all concerned'. One can understand why! At this time 1167 had 95 subscribing members and it was no doubt the reason why, three years later, £50 was set aside from lodge funds to be the first payment for obtaining the present more permanent premises.

In the next few years the lodge settled down in their new home with WBro J. Ferguson WM and Bro J. P. Simpson presenting the VSL which had been used in the old lodge at Wooler (an edition of 1640). Bro M. Wilson was thanked for carving masonic symbols on the corbels of the roof, and a plan by WBro F. H. S. Sitwell, explaining the Constellations depicted on the lodge room ceiling, was handed over for safe keeping.

Such a rich and varied history, with so much left unsaid, needs to be borne in mind as the visitor turns off the street, walks down the length of the present building and turns left into the home of Alnwick Lodge. A sealed Certificate on the wall of the present lodge room, which is reached by turning left once more, expresses the sense of tradition here that is belied by No 1167 only having its

The temple ceiling with actual constellations.

Centenary in 1967. The document reads:

Lux Lucet in Tenebris sed Tenebrae eam non Comprehendunt.

WE the Right Worshipful the Master, Wardens and Secretary of Northumberland Lodge, held at the Beehive in Alnwick, holding of the Grand Lodge in England, do hereby Certify all Regular Lodges, that our Trusty and well beloved brother JAMES SMITH, Linen Draper, of Alnwick aforesaid, was entered an Apprentice, passed a Fellow Craft, and as Recompense due to his Zeal, Diligence, and Capacity, have admitted him into our mysterious secrets of a Master Mason. Given our Hands, and the Seal of the Lodge, this twenty-fourth Day of April 1788.

Thomas Sewell, MASTER
Alex F. Andrew }
Wm. Saunders } WARDENS

Thos. Aiden SECRETARY.
SEAL

Most unusual and certainly striking in this country town lodge is the large and heavily carved sideboard that stands along the west wall of the temple. It at once gives a sense of being a family meeting place and part of the local community whilst also being a proper repository for some of the many treasures that are equally eloquent of a long association with the Craft in these parts. One notices especially a Sunderland Ware Ale Jug inscribed with masonic emblems, silver salvers for use in the first degree ceremony, a small marble pedestal probably used in early Royal Arch ceremonies and bearing interesting masonic symbols, and above all, a Flaming Sword of rather longer length than most and displaying on its hand shield the Sun, Moon and a three-rung ladder. (This should be compared with others mentioned elsewhere in this volume, especially the one at Whitby.) One other feature of this sword is the claymore-style hand-guard which certainly suggests that the otherwise unknown origin of this item was to the north of Alnwick rather than to the the south.

The cushions with their brading and tassels on the three principal pedestals suggest that the design of 1791 has been retained, and in addition this lodge has a further faldstool and pedestal in front of that belonging to the WM. It is on this fourth pedestal that we find the edition of the VSL from 1640 and it is fascinating to turn the pages of this book and see where it was mostly opened in earlier days, and in part still today. The most used pages are those of *Genesis* chapter 4 (the story of Cain and Abel), *Ruth* chapter 2 (the account of how Boaz helped the stranger from afar), *Amos* chapter 7 (where the plumbline is held against the wall) and the Gospel of *St John* chapter 1 (which not only refers to the 'WORD' but also contains those words already seen in the certificate in this hall—'The light shines in the darkness and the darkness could not put it out'). As you turn these revered pages it is not difficult to feel at one with all those many brethren who have held this volume in their hands or placed their hands upon it. Certainly there could be no more solid bond between the past and the present of Alnwick masonry.

The two pedestals at the east have a further feature which is not too common. On that of the Master the sign used is a set square on a shield with a shorter arm to the right and pointing down. On the smaller pedestal used for the obligation is another set square on a black shield only this time the emblem is formed in an upturned V. Compared with the usual square and compasses or the reference to the Euclid theorem one senses here a much older and less sophisticated arrangement. The chairs at the pedestals are of late eighteenth-century origin, not at all elegant but solid and worthy of their purpose and showing in their carving of arms, legs and back real skill by some local craftsman. They were obviously built to last.

On the left wall entering the lodge room there is on a ledge a glass case containing yet more relics of Masonry's local past. Together with four elegant silver jewels for a Master, Wardens and Secretary we find three firing glasses, a barrel-style gavel and poignard, and two die-stamps or hand seals which were obviously of help to the officers of the Northumberland and St Michael's lodges

Alnwick temple showing the east view. The 'flaming' sword is visible on the Master's pedestal. Also of interest is the additional pedestal and the two designs of squares depicted on these.

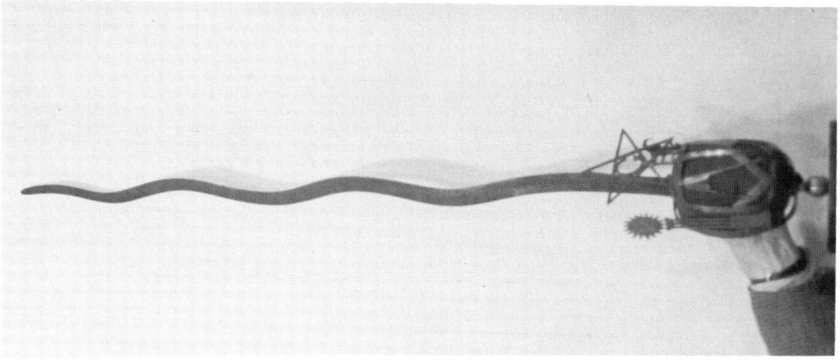

The ancient Claymore-handled wavy tyler's sword.

here. It is in this case that the 1788 Certificate, mentioned above, is normally kept.

We have referred to the remarkable collections of old minutes in Alnwick and these are naturally a treasured possession. There is also, beside the Laudian Bible whose contents we have looked at, another Scottish Bible dating back to 1765, and two copies of Constitutions printed in 1767,stamped 'Alnwick Northumberland Lodge No.419'. We may also be shown a Circular from the Grand Lodge, before the date of adhesive stamps, and bearing the dates 'London 27 December 1817' and 'Newcastle 31 December 1817'. Its contents concern 'Any ideas on improving existing Laws and Regulations' and not only is that still a relevant matter but the speed of the post northwards leaves us with little to crow about in so-called modern days.

Having kept our eyes on the various objects around the walls and floor of the lodge it is worth ending our visit with a consideration of the general lay-out of the whole temple. We lift our eyes to the now much richer ceiling than in Sunday School days. Not only do we find there the stars and their main constellations but a great central circle of the Zodiac creating a true sense of Masonry Universal that bursts beyond this modest but charming northern hall and takes in all those who live beneath that celestial canopy. Our eye will be caught by the two fine pillars which flank the SW's chair albeit occupying the north-west and south-west corners of the lodge carpet. They are somewhat varied from other pillars we have seen. Set on a small black and gold pedestal we see in the SW corner a pillar of the Ionic order bearing a terrestrial globe above it, whilst at the other side we have a Corinthian pillar with the celestial globe above: each of the globes held aloft by a single metal bar that then half surrounds them and holds the central axis of each. Looking west between the pillars one is now aware of the chevy chase sideboard and the lively hunting scene that adorns the whole rear panel of this huge piece against the wall.

Passing out once more through the lodge entrance door a printed sheet caught my eye. It was headed *I AM FREEMASONRY* and its contents are worth reflecting upon:

I AM FREEMASONRY

I was born in antiquity, in the ancient days when men first dreamed of God. I have been tried through the ages, and found true. The crossroads of the World

> bear the imprint of my feet, and the cathedrals of all nations mark the skill of my hands. I strive for beauty and for symmetry. In my heart is wisdom and strength and courage for those who ask. Upon my altars is the Book of Holy Writ, and my prayers are to the One Omnipotent God. My sons work and pray together, without rank or discord, in the public mart and in the inner chamber. By signs and symbols I teach the lessons of life and death, and the relationship of man with God and of man with man. My arms are widespread to receive those of lawful age and good report who seek me of their own free will. I accept them and teach them to use my tools in the building of men, and, thereby, find direction in their own quest for perfection so much desired and so difficult to attain. I lift up the fallen and shelter the sick. I hark to the orphan's cry, the widow's tears, the pain of the old and destitute. I am not church, nor party, nor school, yet my sons bear a full share of responsibility to God, to country, to neighbour and themselves. They are freemen, tenacious of their liberties and alert to lurking danger. At the end I commit them as each one undertakes the journey beyond the vale into the glory of everlasting life. I ponder the sand within the glass and think how small is a single life in the eternal Universe. Always have I taught immortality, and even as I raise men from darkness into Light, I am a way of life. I am Freemasonry.
>
> (Ray V. Denslow)

In this memorable northern temple we touch on a past kept alive in a simple but fascinating fashion. The passer-by may know nothing of what this building means but the informed visitor will soon realise that here is enshrined what Freemasonry is, and has for long been, about.

BARTON-UPON-HUMBER

On the Banks of the Humber

"ON 14 AUGUST 1816 the Revd George Oliver, Vicar of Clee, PM of the Apollo Lodge No 544 of Great Grimsby and Prov Grand Chaplain of the County (*sic*) of Lincoln preached a Sermon at St Peter's Church, Barton-upon-Humber as part of a Provincial Meeting of the United Grand Lodge." So runs a portion of the title page of the booklet produced after that occasion in Barton-upon-Humber, and its retention by the occupants of the present Masonic Hall there emphasise both their own love of tradition and the long-standing presence of Freemasonry in that town and district.

Indeed, it will not be irrelevant to our theme if but a brief extract from that sermon is given as showing the link between what was said 170 years ago and what is still preserved in the hall that is the home of Barton-upon-Humber Masonry today.

Starting with the text from 1 *Corinthians*, chapter 10 and part of verse 31: 'Whatsoever ye do—do all to the glory of God', Mr Oliver (only later Dr) moved swiftly into his theme. 'The Foundation of Masonry, is Religion. He who attempts to build a system of Masonry on any *other* foundation,—like the foolish man who built his house on sand,—will find his labours subject to dissolution, from every gust of opposition—every breeze of ridicule. But erected on *this* rock, it will withstand the rude assaults of every fierce invader! Unmoved amidst the tumultuous waves of persecution, it rears its venerable head, and shines like a beacon amidst the impenetrable darkness with which it is surrounded.

Three of the six shields presented to the lodge in 1883. These depict (left to right), *pillars and archstone with cubic altar; an open book; and the Moon with seven stars.*

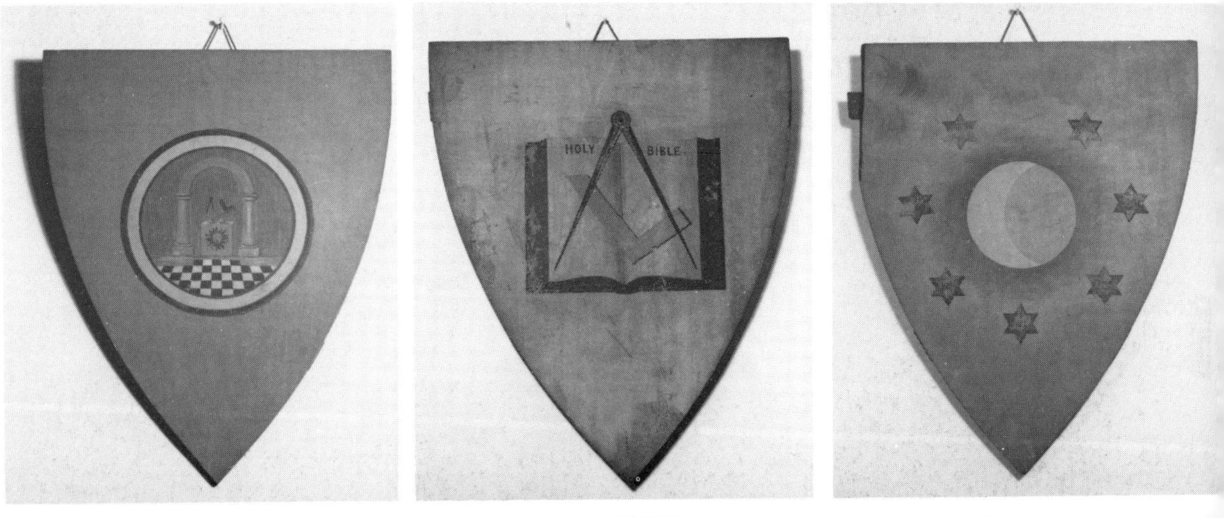

'The Secrets of this truly valuable Art, are of a nature so consonant with the mysteries of Christianity, that whoever is possessed of the sublimities of the former, cannot be deficient in the practice of the latter . . .' He added in a footnote, 'it has ever been my firm opinion, that NO MAN CAN BE A GOOD MASON, WHO IS NOT A GOOD CHRISTIAN'.

It was the author of this address who was to refer in another sermon that year to the Revd Matthew Barnett as 'the Father of Masonry in Lincolnshire'. Those who gathered on 21 September, 1787 to constitute the Old St Matthew's Lodge at Barton (in the house of Bro John Morley known by the name of the George Inn) may indeed have wanted to honour their first Worshipful Master, who was then a 26-years old schoolmaster, but it is equally likely that they took the title from the festival on which the ceremony was conducted—St Matthew's Day. On that occasion the founders first heard an oration from Matthew Barnett, but then also proceeded to St Peter's to hear a sermon by the Revd Thomas Robinson. By December the lodge numbered 23 persons and was still the only masonic lodge in the whole of Lincolnshire; and in 1808 a sum of 5 guineas was voted to assist British prisoners of war in France. The lodge met twice a month in winter and once a month in the summer and the Installation was on St Matthew's Day—not, it may be noticed, on St John's.

Preserved in the archives of the present hall and framed on one of its walls is a receipted bill for the original furniture of the old lodge—'a mallet and two truncheons, Mosaick pavement, 2 Dorick colums, windows blinds, three mahogany chairs and a bolt for the door' being among them. Certainly the furniture we see today is directly linked in part with this list for we know that the Bible, Master and Wardens' chairs, the main pedestal, candlesticks, columns and ballot box were recovered from a tenant of the George Inn just before 1873 when the new St Matthew's Lodge, No 1447, was warranted.

In that interval the first Master, Matthew Barnett, became DepPGM of Lincolnshire. The last entry of an initiation was in 1825 when Bro George Capes, a draper in the town, was in the chair, and eleven other members were admitted as joining brethren. The last cash count was in 1836 and though three comedies were

The inlay decoration of the Worshipful Master (left) *and Senior Warden Chairs. These show the sun rising and setting.*

performed at the Theatre in Barton-upon-Humber 'under the patronage of the WM Officers and Brethren of the Lodge' in June 1839, the lodge began to decline and was erased in 1851.

One fascinating item still kept at the hall today is a precious booklet printed at Hull in 1826 and entitled, *Reminiscences of Free Masonry; or Scripture Illustrations of that Sublime Ancient, and Honourable Order.... The whole collected and arranged for the information, instruction, and improvement of the Members of the Saint Matthew's Lodge, No.488, Barton-upon-Humber, BY GEORGE CAPES, W.M.* It is a fascinating piece of instruction. Let me quote but three extracts:

> ... the secrets of the brotherhood, if revealed, would appear to the world as indistinct and scattered fragments,—whilst they convey to Masons, an uniform and well-connected system.
>
> Our antiquity is in our principles, maxims, languages, and religion; those we derive from Eden, from the patriarchs, and from the sages of the East; all of which are made perfect under the Christian dispensation.

A view of the temple looking from east to west. The VSL is displayed on a separate pedestal in front of the WM's. The desk in the right foreground is for the secretary.

> The young Mason may safely and conscientiously permit the perusal of this publication to any of his friends not of the order. . . . He will thereby prove, to a demonstration, that, at all our meetings, religion is acknowledged as the basis of our order, and the sacred law considered as the unerring standard of truth and justice, which regulates our actions by the precepts it contains.

To see the furniture and in some measure to associate with the author of such exquisite sense cannot but make the visit to the hall at Barton a delight. Its contents, as we shall see, bear out the 'religious' influences that have affected the masons of Barton-upon-Humber from the outset of any lodge here.

The first founders and members of the 'new' Matthew's Lodge met at the Volunteers Hall but we are told that when in 1875 a very old masonic picture was presented to the lodge by a Bro T. Fuller it was not allowed to stay in the hall, as not being secure, and it was placed in the care of Bro J. Sissons, one of the officers. That same year steps were taken to find a better and more satisfactory 'home' and £50 was paid to Major Uppleby for the purchase of some land adjoining the Brigg

Looking east clearly showing the marble chequered platforms for the pedestals and, behind the WM's chair, the two long panels containing the Lord's Prayer, the Ten Commandments and the Creed as set out in the Anglican Book of Common Prayer.

Road but near the centre of town. Shares of up to £360 were taken out in one evening and eight brethren as Trustees were set up, to act as a Building Committee. Within three months a foundation stone was laid in the presence of 106 brethren and their attendance led to the following write-up in the *Hull and Lincolnshire Times*, 22 May.

> The novelty of the spectacle of so many members of the Craft in full Masonic attire attracted a considerable amount of attention and curiosity on the part of the outside public, and the procession was accompanied to the site of the building by a large crowd of persons.

There were several presentations that same year for the lodge furniture and we can see the assembled results of these presentations in the lay-out of the lodge today. They adorn a simple and not overlarge upper room in a building which has no external decoration whatsoever and which thus exemplifies the taciturnity and proper 'secrecy' to which Barton-upon-Humber masons have ever been so strictly directed. Within the simple entrance the century old hall begins to reveal its country style and function—its half-panelled dining room with trestle tables, its winding stairs and lodge room above.

The religious nature of the latter is immediately obvious for on the east wall behind a simple raised dais are two panels—one containing the Lord's Prayer and the Ten Commandments, and the other the Creed as set out in the Anglican Book of Common Prayer. (It would be interesting to know if, as I suspect, this is the only masonic place in which such an item appears). There too hangs the original, Victorian silk banner of the lodge showing St Matthew pointing to the gospel book held in his left hand. The visitor attending a lodge meeting here would also notice that the Chaplain had his own distinctive collar and silver jewel.

The chequered flooring of the lodge is not provided by a carpet but by beautifully inlaid marble tiling and just below the dais to left and right are the two special desks, handsomely carved and with two crossed keys on the front for the Treasurer, whilst the Secretary's desk has, of course, two crossed quill pens. Also very evident is a large gong for the use in ceremonies, especially in the third degree. There are also six shields bearing masonic symbols that were presented to the lodge in 1883 by the then IPM, WBro W. Heseltine. These illustrate the Sun (with full face and rays); a Crescent Moon with seven stars in a circle around (and the unlit area of the moon also appears); the Holy Bible (*sic*) opened with a set square in blue and superimposed dividers on the open pages; a tripod of three poles bound at the top with the rope bearing a pulley and clamp that hold a square ashlar between them; and a circle of gold surrounding a scene in which two simple pillars bearing a quite plain arch (without keystone) stand on a platform up to which runs a chequered pavement. Between the pillars stands a cubic altar with a sun's face and rays on its front and above it two figures that look like a harp and a dove (possibly meaning harmony and peace). They certainly add materially to the overall character of this modest provincial lodge room.

Yet it is the three main officers' chairs that must claim our special attention. That of the WM stands impressively on the dais and has carved into the back of it three Latin phrases:

FAC AEQUITATEM (Do Justice)
AMA CLEMENTIAM (Love Mercy)
ET AMBULA MODESTE CUM DEO (and walk humbly with God)

but onto the back has been superimposed a further panel showing a rising sun in lapis lazuli and the words 'Let there be light', from the book of Genesis.

The chairs of the Wardens do not have any Latin upon them but they too have similar representations of the sun in the same precious stone. That of the Senior Warden shows a setting sun and has the words 'Walk as children of light' from the Epistle to the Ephesians, whilst that of the Junior Warden shows a sun in full splendour and is accompanied by the words 'And the darkness comprehended it not' from the opening chapter of St John's Gospel. Upon the latter two pedestals there are inscriptions commemorating the laying of the foundation stone and the consecration of the lodge respectively.

The general feeling of someone who comes to this unassuming but well-preserved temple must surely be one of respect and admiration for the evident faith and fidelity which have preserved, unseen, so manifest a link with masonry in these parts over just 200 years. The gentle shade of blue on the walls, the charming and well-kept organ presented in 1940, the ballot box with 'Pro' and 'Con', and the collecting-for-charity box that is an upturned maul, together with an intriguing masonic chart upon the temple wall, all combine to make this a place for the visitor to remember. In every sense there is more here than at first meets the eye but the overall effect is one that will give any brother lasting pleasure.

In the collection of valued items to which this hall and its occupants is heir there is one more relic from the past which needs mention. It is a simple paper-bound booklet with charred lower edges and entitled *Account of the Present State of the St. Matthew's Lodge, No.488, Barton-upon-Humber: with Observations on Freemasonry*.... It was printed in Barton in AD 1819, AL 5823. From pages 13 and 14 and the title pages there are two passages that might well convey so much that this hall has sought to retain and prove.

> Did the essence of MASONRY consist in the knowledge of *particular secrets* or *peculiar forms*, it might be alleged that our amusements were trifling and superficial. But this is not the case; they are only the *keys* to our treasure, and having their use, are preserved; while, from the recollection of the lessons which they inculcate, the well-informed Mason derives instruction; he draws them to a near inspection, views them through a proper medium, adverts to the circumstances which gave them rise, and dwells upon the tenets they convey. Finding them replete with useful information, he prizes them as sacred . . .

Let every Mason here below
Our Noble Science here improve;
'Twill raise his soul to realms above,
And make this Lodge,—a Lodge of LOVE.

BERWICK

The Border Hall of Berwick

We the Master Wardens and Secretary of the Lo. of St. George No.70 Berwick Do hereby certify to all whom it may concern that *JOHN BEST* was regularly Entered an Apprentice, Passed Fellow Craft and as a Recompence due to his Zeal, Diligence and Capacity We have raised him to the Degree of a MM. We therefore in the strongest manner Recommend him to every place of Trust in Masonry And that all Regular, Constituted Lodges in Ancient Masonry may receive him as a trusty and well beloved Brother and Render him every service as far as the Rules of Masonry direct

Given under our hand
(Signed)

Here at once in the showcase of the temple at Berwick upon Tweed is clear evidence of the antiquity of the Freemasonry long practised in and around this Hall. The above certificate is dated 12 December, 1777, and is a fine and legible example of the lodge certificates issued in the days before the formal ones from London which are now so generally familiar to us. Its presence here is a sure indication of what other treasures we shall find as we wander through these premises.

Indeed, in the very next alcove of the dining room the visitor will see a couple of ancient cases containing two well-preserved forked pennants. They are in remarkably good condition and bear a most interesting description: 'These banners were reputed to have been sent from Wark-on-Tweed to Berwick for safe keeping during the unsettled times which culminated in the Battle of Flodden 1513.' To the mason who has any interest in the Order of the Temple they represent a significant attraction even though their provenance was long before any possible connection with Masonic Knighthood.

It is such items as these that await the visitor to the Masonic Hall in the centre of this Border town. At first sight he could be forgiven for imagining that it was just another chapel, for the principal feature of the main façade is a large ecclesiastical style window with stone tracery, though on more careful examination one notices that above the two lower pointed lights the upper part of this space is filled with a circular ring of stone enclosing the intertwined triangles that we know as the Seal of Solomon. The same motif is repeated above the window at the apex of the gabled roof so that there can be no mistake for the initiated as to what this building is. Below the window there is a blue door with a fanlight, over which is a carved stone scroll bearing the tell-tale words, Aude, Vide, Tace, and flanking the scroll and attached midway up the wall are two decorated columns. These form the base for two niches that have, further above them, the kinds of canopy that would cover a statue beneath. As there is nothing there today it is a matter for conjecture as to whom the architect would have sought to place there. Could it perhaps have been Moses and Solomon?

How did this hall come to be built, for that it was made for the purpose there can be no question? As the home of St David's Lodge (presently No 393) it owed its eventual erection to the frustration increasingly felt by members of that lodge during the years after its being warranted in 1828. The lodge had in fact been constituted in 1773 and a contemporary poem gives a vivid account of the event. A few of the verses are worth recording—

The Master's pedestal with overhead canopy.

But see the music does advance,
With measured step as if to dance,
  Their number three times three;
Next comes the Master of the band,
And next the Tyler, sword in hand,
  Like knight of chivalry.

With all St. David's at his back,
All decently array'd in black,
  With gloves and aprons white.
With ribbons trimm'd of crimson dye,
And sashes edg'd, that to the eye,
  Present a pleasant sight.

The Officers their badges wear,
Those out of office medals fair,
  And hand in hand they move.
By this the world may plainly see,
That the cement of Masonry,
  Is sweet fraternal love.

The lovely youths too quickly pass,
I scarce discern each well-known face,
  Til from my sight they're fled.
Next comes Ford Lodge, a jovial crew,
With gloves and aprons trimm'd with blue,
  And sashes edg'd with red.

With flags display'd with blue and gold,
Which are most charming to behold,
  They walk with decent pace;
In them both strength and beauty shine,
  Emblems of Masonry divine,
  And every manly grace.

But now St. Cuthbert's come in view,
With yellow edge their liv'ries blue,
  St. George's now appear,
In blue and white edg'd liveries clad,
  With proper emblems of their trade
  The Masters close the rear.

To church they go, this is well done,
Well thrives the work that's well begun;
  But mark the preacher's theme;
He tells them how fraternal love
In every situation which they move,
  Will keep them free from Blame.

The service done, the jovial crew,
Walk to the Lodge in order due,
  And pair and pair ascend;
Thou perched upon the Master's chair,
Shalt see the mighty doings there,
  And thy assistance lend.

The dinner done, the toasts go round,
The bells do ring, the music sound
  To celebrate the day:
The loving Brethren all agree
  To sing in praise of Masonry
    And pass the hours away.

The lodge first met at the Berwick Arms and it is worth noting that during their ten years there they once more proceeded in 1830 to the Parish Church to honour the passing of 'his late Gracious Majesty George the Fourth' and in 1833 attended the funeral of one of the Founders of the Lodge at Tweedmouth Churchyard.

By 1838 they felt it desirable to move to the 'Hen and Chickens' Inn at Sandgate but by 1840 they had passed on to the 'Salmon'. In 1850 they tried the experiment of renting a private room in Sandgate but within 5 years it was again proving too expensive and back to the 'Salmon' they went. Thus they wandered about until at last Bro George Moor, initiated in 1865, moved in 1871 'that immediate and active steps be taken to raise funds for the erection of a new suitable and commodious Lodge Room.' The first Committee was formed.

Several unsuccessful attempts to find a plot at last resulted in the present one being discovered and it was resolved 'that the sum of £80 be offered for the eligible site at the corner of Walkergate Lane'. The final price was in fact £95.

In the month of October 1872 an attempt was made to obtain the services of HRH the Prince of Wales to lay the foundation stone of the building but his medical advisors dissuaded him and in any case the Prov GM was also abroad at this time 'being compelled by indisposition to visit the sunny climes of Southern Europe'. 'The process of erection was proceeded with', says a lodge history, as they dispensed with the laying of a foundation stone, and such rapid progress was made that by 30 January, 1874 the Deputy PGM was able to carry out the ceremony of dedication. At the dinner in the Kings Arms Assembly Rooms afterwards 80 brethren sat down.

The care and attention lavished by these Border masons on their new hall is evidenced by several facts. In 1877 it was estimated that the total cost of building and furnishing the Hall had been £1900 but that already £1200 had been paid off. At this point a Bro A. J. Forbes, to commemorate his year in the Chair presented both a crimson carpet and a tessellated pavement, whilst Bro Moor the instigator of the whole scheme, completed the floor covering by the gift of a crimson skin rug. In 1877 the stairs were also carpeted and a matting put down for the passage and vestibule. In 1880 an organ was bought for £66, and by 1883 only £250 remained of the original debt. In 1888 they were clear. What had been achieved was fully revealed when, in their report that year, the lodge committee pointed out that only 20 years before the balance against the lodge had been £1 13s 2½d!

It is not surprising that there continues to be a sense of high regard for their inheritance from the past among the brethren today and it is soon evident to an interested visitor why this should be so. One has only to enter the front door to be at once confronted with yet another well-preserved relic of the ancient practice of Freemasonry in this Border town. It is a two sided banner in a swivel case, bearing the name St. Cuthbert's Lodge No.133 and carrying in the top left corner of the front face the following inscription woven in gold letters on a red base:

> "A GIFT from the BRETHREN of the VIII or King's Regt. to St. Cuthbert's Lodge No.133. Jas. Weatherhead Master 1806".

The banner is clearly that of an Antients' lodge as can be seen from the Coat of Arms on this same side being that of the Antients Grand Lodge. Above the outstretched wings of the Cherubim over the Ark of the Covenant are two hands clasping each other, whilst above the lodge's name is a Pentacle. To the left of the Arms is a Blazing Sun and to the right a Crescent Moon with a face, the whole being surrounded by an array of oak or acacia leaves. The compasses and square are shown at the foot in the Fellow Craft position.

On the reverse side the Pentacle, the lodge title and leaves are all the same but the sun and moon are reversed and the square and compasses at the foot are now

The Masonic Hall at Berwick built in 1874.

The impressive organ and pillars in the east.

as in the third degree. The picture in the centre of the banner is now of RA significance with an arch over two pillars but a ray of light darting from an All-seeing Eye in the clouds above and piercing the arch to illuminate first a letter G, and then below that a red cross above an open pair of tablets representing the Ten Commandments before which stands a crowned figure in a red tunic. He stands on a mosaic pavement above five steps and at the corners of the bottom step are two masons with black jackets and large white embroidered aprons. Beneath them and the bottom step are the words—

SIT LUX ET LUX FUIT

Finally, behind the red square on the other side, and thus in the top right hand corner here, is a Garter Blue circlet with strap bearing the words "Let this be our Standard" and enclosing a collection of a drum, musical instruments and two flags, one of them the Union Jack. As an introduction to any masonic building it is most striking and here it underlines the measure of the items preserved for posterity.

Passing from the vestibule into the corridor that leads to the dining room one becomes aware of the simple, homespun nature of the building and then one enters what is as much a museum as a place for the after proceedings. The two items first mentioned in this chapter belong here and they are flanked by many other memorabilia. Here is a Harper certificate of 1810 for one Thomas Hindlaugh of Lodge St George's No 70. There is also a Harper RA certificate of 1807 for John Johnston showing the broken arch and the Cherubim again bending over the Ark on the pedestal. There is a small mallet used by the DC at the Festive Board of St David's Lodge No 393 and presented by Bro Walter P. Carr at Easter 1902. It bears an inscription: 'This mallet made from the Oak beams of the Old Kilwinning lodge being part of the wreck of the Spanish Armada. Ex.Bro. W.F. Shaw.'

In one of the simple show cases is a copy of the marble tablet found in 1906 at the N.E. corner of Tweedmouth church. The inscription here reads:

> "This Church Foundation was laid Decr 27th 1782 by the R^{t} Worp^{l}, M^{r}, Salby Morton of the Lo. of St. Cuthbert No 133
> Mr Thos. Pearson Ja^{s} Ramsey. Ch, Warden^{s}.
>
> A–A Scul^{t}"

Alongside this further connection with the banner in the entrance hall we see an old Tyler's hat (such as is also referred to in the hall at Bolton). It is a fine example of this once regular headgear. Whilst beside this example of early nineteenth century usage is a board on the room's mantelpiece which reads:

> "June 1902. Berwick on Tweed Masonic Club.
> Whisky 5d per glass
> Brandy 8d " "
> Sherry 5d " "
> Claret 4d " "
> Bottled Beer 2d " "

Certainly the most impressive item, partly because it is so often used at the table and also because of its age, is a plain oak armchair with modest carving at its head and the inscription I.D. 1733. The Master sits in this seat with real pride to preside over the entertaining of the brethren.

It is more than time to move upstairs. We do so by a veritable winding staircase that leads to a narrow landing. The walls of the staircase and landing are covered with further intriguing items—a picture of James Weatherhead who was named on the St Cuthbert's banner; of Robert Ord, PM of St. David's Lodge (then numbered 554); a certificate bearing the names of Kelly,GM, Anson,DepGM, and L. Dermott with the seal of the Antients Grand Lodge; an exquisitely preserved RA apron which shows not only Aaron's rod but the three Principals all wearing their once accustomed Crown, Turban and Mitre (and as can be seen in the halls at Leicester, Manchester and Bristol); and of particular interest a framed, 10 foot high tracing board for the second degree with an unusual design—the upper portion showing a rainbow spanning the Sun and Crescent Moon (both with faces) and a star and all-seeing eye between them, with an open volume of the VSL upon which are the square and compasses in the position of the Fellow Craft. Below this upper panel which covers only a third of the board we see a typical eighteenth century replica of the Temple of three main storeys with a tower and gabled roof above it and a figure standing in its doorway at the top of a large flight of 15 steps with two other figures at the left and right corners below. The whole of the steps and building are flanked by two enormous pillars looking at first sight like two minarets but clearly being B and J with their globes and nets. At the foot of the pillars are three grand steps which complete the whole. It is a Tracing Board which appears nowhere else and it will be of special interest one day to discover its date of origin.

We now pass into the lodge room itself with its lofty timbered roof, the large metal G at the centre and on the blue ceiling the representation of the stars at night. As we move from the west end we are bound to notice the well-preserved pipe organ facing the Master but with a draped curtain to veil the organist from view. It was in 1897 that the brethren decided that the earlier portable instrument which they had bought was not in keeping with the lodge room and building and so they spent £160 on this present piece. Within three years the organ debt was wholly cleared.

Before the organ stand two metal pillars bearing two sizeable blue globes. The golden-coloured pillars have well carved, grey wooden bases which are mounted on three square steps. These are copies of the original pillars used in the St. Cuthbert's Lodge No 133 and one of these was found only a decade ago in a garden at Tweedmouth where it still lies. They have been beautifully 'restored' and now add to the grace and authenticity of this temple. Their use here only completes the impression made by the same lodge's banner on our entry. Between the pillars stands the SW's chair with its richly carved back and the date 1647. The WM's chair is of almost identical design but has some additional implements (the axe and the square) and also bears the date 1647.

Just to the right of the SW is the place of the JW, so positioned because this lodge room has retained its original chimney piece and clock. The JW's chair is itself of real interest for its back is composed of an arrangement of two broad plumblines as back props with a large level at the base and a decorated centrepiece above. The arms and legs are richly carved and rounded and the seat is of ample proportions. Here and before the other principal officers the pedestals are most gracefully carved with that before the WM being specially so. Before moving to the east it is worth noting that all round the temple there are painted roundels on the upper walls and to the left of the organ, and over the door used solely for the entry of the candidate, there is a KT emblem showing two knights on the one horse bearing one shield and two lances, the whole surrounded by the words +SIG. MILIT. XPISTI. IN. ANGLIA.

In the east we notice that the Secretary and Treasurer have desks at the left and right ends of the three gentle steps that lead up to the canopied dais that stretches the whole length of the east wall. The lodge history puts it like this: 'One would have thought that by (1903) everything possible had been done for the beautifying of the temple and the comfort of the Brethren that it was possible to do, but not so, for in 1905 a Past Masters' Canopy was erected in the Lodge Room.' As can be seen the work was done with the thoroughness already evinced by these Berwick brethren. The seating under this canopy, with the exception of the WM's chair, is entirely uniform with each chair having distinctive headpieces and on some the symbols of office (IPM, Chaplain, etc). The Master's place is marked by two slender pillars and a simple arch around his pedestal, whilst in front of his pedestal desk there is also another pedestal of white stone with its cushion and book, for it is here that candidates take their obligation. The panelled rear of the dais bears an impressive array of warrants, centenary and Royal Arch.

As we turn and prepare to leave this haven of masonic lore at our most northerly border we can notice that same intricate window which first attracted our notice outside. In 1893 WBro Crow, who then redecorated this room, had cathedral glass inserted to still further enhance its glory. His efforts were not in vain. His successors appreciate their inheritance.

BEVERLEY

The Hall in the Shadow of a Minster

To DISCOVER THE origins of masonry in any place is a matter of profound interest to the freemasons who live and work there. In a town with as ancient a history as that of Beverley in the Province of the North and East Riding the first intimations of the Craft might be expected to have been especially early. In actual fact this is not quite the case, at least not in comparison with some of the other places that are visited in this volume and the others in the series. It is true that there was a regimental lodge No 442—later 336 and 450—St George's East York Militia—which seems to have found a home for a decade around its headquarters in this town, but it then moved on again to Beccles in Suffolk. It is true that it occasionally met in Beverley once or twice more in the next 30 years but in 1829 it was erased and its warrant passed on to another lodge.

Nonetheless, though this could not in a sense be called a local lodge, it did meet for that decade in and around Beverley—at the Sign of the Golden Ball (or the Black Bull) and during its sojourn here some civilians seemed to have joined and some of the military personnel left it to remain in the area when it moved on. At any rate the first local Freemasonry of St John started only when the regimental lodge had passed to East Anglia. In 1793 a warrant under the auspices of the Premier or Moderns Grand Lodge was granted and Constitutional Lodge No 525 was established, to meet at the same Golden Ball that had housed the 'military brethren'. It is interesting to note from the first minute book that St George's Lodge at Beccles is described as 'our Mother Lodge'.

It was right of course that Beverley should be host to St John's Masonry. Nothing is more likely to leave a lasting impression on the mind of the visitor to this town than the magnificent Gothic minster which is really the collegiate church of St John. As one authority has said, 'For architectural beauty it compares with York Minster itself' and it is something of a surprise for anyone who might come upon the town unawares to see rising from amongst its ancient streets and houses this vast, towered pile that seems so huge for such a modest place. When, however, you find that it is by no means the only church of interest and distinction, that there is a grammar school whose foundation is of such antiquity that its exact date is unknown, and that there are many houses of special grace and beauty from the mediaeval period onwards, you realise that this is a place in which builders and masons can rightly take great pride.

Before we come to the Masonic Hall, that might be rightly thought to have much to live up to, it will be important for us to trace something of the history of this Constitutional Lodge whose home it is and which has continued unceasingly for what is now almost 200 years. It is a story that begins with the first initiate being a joiner (if that doesn't sound like a contradiction) and one of the founders being the Reader at the Minster. In the same month as the warrant was issued two candlesticks were purchased which can still be seen in the room used by the Past Masters.

In May 1793 it was decided to do two things—one was to frame the Constitution *and* glaze it, and the other was to approve the date of Consecration as being St John's Day (how could it be any other?). On 7 June they made even more decisions—to have the Highland Band for the procession, to pay the Singers ½ guinea for the Occasional Hymns or Anthems, and to have the bells only chime in with the band music as otherwise they might drown the musicians! They felt that this was best because that is what happened each Sunday!

The consecration was marked by a sermon at St Mary's by the Provincial Grand Chaplain, the lodge meeting and its consecration proper by a Past Deputy PGM, and £16 3s 2d spent on the whole of the occasion—singers, dinners, drink, waiters and broken glasses all included. At last the Constitutional Lodge was officially launched and whilst it must have been as eager as we are today to avoid political discussion in our proceedings its name, like that of its earlier namesake No 55, probably meant that it was eager to assert its anti-Jacobite *and* anti-Jacobin opinions to those in authority.

The magnificent feature of Beverley masonic hall is the arcade behind the Master's chair, with keystone and painted rays. From the ceiling is suspended a letter 'G' with irradiated circle above.

Within the year the lodge was already in a new venue at the Tyger Inn though it was to stay here for 55 years. In 1795 we have the first mention of the lodge needing finance to help defray the cost of decorating and furnishing the lodge. It was furniture of which they could be justly proud and which we shall examine more carefully in a little while. In 1796 they celebrated St John the Baptist's Day by a procession to the Minster where the Rev Bethell Robinson preached the sermon and their first chaplain, the Rev Thomas Rogers, took the service as minister there.

By 1813 there is mention of a new chair for the Worshipful Master, whilst in 1821, on the occasion of celebrating the Coronation of George IV, the previous Grand Master of the Craft, the WM of the day provided 'new Blue Hangings for the Jewels of the officers, and Bro S. W. Fletcher (was) ordered to clean, gild and paint the Regalia of the lodge. (As we have seen in other halls the term 'regalia' meant many other items than simply the clothing of the brethren). A handsome seal bearing RA masonic emblems was presented to the lodge in 1822 by Bro R. Mackenzie Beverley, Deputy Provincial Grand Master, who, though he was elected a joining member, was also elected as WM the same evening! That seal is still on view in the present premises and marks yet another link between the lodge's present and its past.

It was this same R. M. Beverley who chaired a committee as early as 1823 to examine the possibility of having a separate lodge room built for that purpose, but nothing obviously came of the matter either then or in 1836 under Bro Phillips, WM and it was to be another century before that dream was realised. Meanwhile they at last acquired two new jewels—for the Inner and Outer Guard—and also began to acquire the basis of a lodge library by subscribing to 'a work lately advertised by Bro Oliver of the Grimsby Lodge, containing Lectures on the Masonic Symbols'.

When the Tyger Inn was closed as a hostelry the dispensation to meet there also ceased and it was only because Bro Tuting of North Bar Street cared for the furniture and allowed the members to gather at his home that the lodge was preserved to eventually meet in the Assembly rooms. When it did so at last in 1849 Bro Tuting was given one sovereign for his trouble.

A presentation was now made to the lodge which had left its imprint on the temple we are yet to enter. It is a very special large 'Flaming Sword' which is now placed near the pedestal of the Worshipful Master. It was given by a Bro West in August 1853 and there is some likelihood that it may have been a legacy of the earlier Militia Lodge which had been 'stored' and was now brought to light. Of its age and authenticity there can be no doubt as a comparison of it with others we have seen in this volume (Alnwick and Bolton) will clearly prove. A description of the present sword was once provided by Bro T. Foley, a PM:

'The Sword so fixed in our Lodge is a large flaming double-edged sword; the Blade 3 ft 1 in long, the Hilt 7 in total length 3 ft 8 in. It is fixed in a wooden stand, painted and gilt, the lower part having three steps to which are attached two Gilt Columns on square bases; the 47th Proposition between the columns and this surmounted by a Circular Arch to which the hilt of the sword is secured; it is regularly placed . . . close to the position of the SD and remains with its naked blade uplifted during the time the lodge is at Masonic work'.

There can be no doubt that this was formerly the shape of the Tyler's sword and its replacement by any ordinary sword is merely a matter of convenience or plain ignorance. This type of sword refers naturally to that flaming sword which was represented in mediaeval times as that of the angel set to guard the entrance to Paradise and from which Adam and Eve were dismissed. The presence still of this sword in the Beverley Masonic Hall is yet one more link with a freemasonry of more than two centuries ago even if there may not be many who fully appreciate its real significance.

In 1885 a further committee took up the matter of whether, when the Beverley Dispensary in Register Square would become vacant, it could be suitably adapted for use by the brethren. Other houses were also considered by the committee but in 1886 it seemed that the first option was possible. It was to be the lodge's home for another 40 years. It was dedicated by the Hon W. S. Orde-Powlett, Deputy Prov GM, on 21 December and most of the £348 required for the alterations were immediately met by contributions from the brethren.

The possession of much more secure and roomy property meant that a new spate of gifts came into the lodge's possession. On 6 January 1887 WBro Goulding contributed two further bibles so that from that date until now the custom has been retained of having a VSL on the Wardens' as well as the Master's pedestal. WBro E. Bryan also presented the very fine celestial and terrestrial globes, secured by brass rings but supported by much taller tripod frames than usual, their overall height being about three and a half feet. In the present hall they stand in the north-east and south-east corners of the temple but it is likely that when first procured they were placed on the floor of the lodge in place of the usual floor pillars.

The centenary warrant of the Constitutional Lodge now so proudly displayed in the present hall reminds the visitor that in that year the lodge was singularly proud to have the Rt Hon the Earl of Londesborough, Past Grand Warden of England as

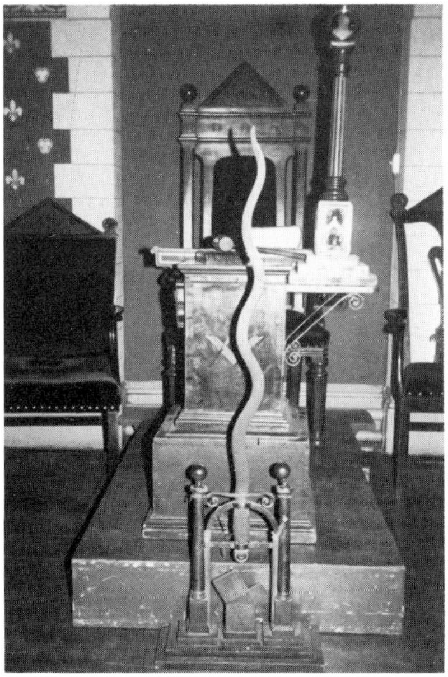

The entrance to Beverley hall with unusual but distinctive masonic emblem. Right: *The Master's pedestal in front of which stands the wavy sword and supporting stand.*

the Worshipful Master. It was a year specially marked by the presentation of the very handsome solid silver Loving Cup which was presented by the brethren of Liberty Lodge, Beverly, Massachusetts, USA. They did this 'in remembrance of the common origin to which the name bears witness, and as a token of fraternal fellowship and national amity'. The cup has three handles, weighs 55 oz and is about 8 in. high.

In presenting the cup on behalf of the American brethren the lodge Secretary described how two years before one of their members had written to him asking for a stone from the ruins of Beverley Minster as a rough ashlar for their lodge. A stone was sent from some kept for repairs but he had to assure the Americans that for once their Minster was not a relic of Henry VIII's depradations but was very much a working church building.

As a further memento of this year the Earl of Londesborough gave to Constitutional Lodge a perfect copy of the lovely banner he had sent to the Liberty Lodge in the USA. It carried the Beverley (Yorks) coat of arms with Ionic and Corinthian columns as its frame. Lord Londesborough's personal motto *Adversa virtute repello* (I counter misfortunes with valour) was above a scroll giving Constitutional Lodge's name, with a Bible bearing a square and compasses below. It was designed by WBro Thomson Foley, who gave the description of the old sword above. Lord Londesborough also presented 4 dozen firing glasses to commemorate the Queen's Diamond Jubilee and a similar number were dispatched to Massachusetts.

By 1917 a sum of £50 was set aside towards the necessary Building Fund that would be required when the lease on the current Masonic Hall ran out in 1927.

A view of the Warden's pedestals with the Ashlars positioned in front of each. The Tracing Boards are behind the closed curtains on the south side.

More volumes were added to the collection being created for the lodge library and in 1918 WBro J. G. Wallis gave the brethren an antique porcelain jug which was of Liverpool ware and probably 150 years old. The donor had been particularly struck by the design on the jug's side which almost exactly paralleled that first Woodcut made by Mr Michael Carrall, a Printer, for the lodge summonses in 1806. Bro Elwell offered to make a cabinet to keep the jug in and this is still a part of lodge furniture.

For the 125th Anniversary Bro Hugh Stephenson handed over an old Certificate and apron that had belonged to his great-grandfather, grandfather and father, all of whom had been initiated in the Constitutional Lodge. Another committee started to look at the prospects for another building and in 1926 the recommendation to build was accepted. The United Methodist Chapel in Trinity Lane was available for about £1000 with a further sum of about £1500–£2000 for essential alterations. By 16 September the negotiation was complete and with the assistance of the Mayor and the Medical Officer of Health a very temporary stay in the school clinic tided them over until they could start in the present hall.

Thus it was that just 60 years ago this hall, with all its contents that linked it in close association with the people and century that had gone before, was opened for use. A piano appeared, three oak carving chairs and 53 dining chairs as at present in the dining room, and even silver salt cellars for the dining table, were given or bought. The lodge was invited to attend service at the Minster by the Chaplain, the Rev Bro W. H. Rigg, and this was repeated in 1930. Mrs Foley presented a showcase containing the Masonic clothing, jewels and certificates of her husband and the present set of gavels and maul (not to mention an india-rubber one for a certain purpose, that had come earlier) were made from old oak which had been removed from the roof of St Mary's, Beverley, after a necessary restoration there.

Standing then, as one can now do, on the south side of St John's Minster and looking away from the church towards the station an area of open ground now permits you to see the end of Trinity Street. Down it, on the right, stands the fine façade of what was once the chapel. Today it is markedly a Masonic Hall, for apart from the four Corinthian pilasters that grace its frontage there is a double-leaved front door in blue and above it a plinth bearing a circle in which a square and compasses lie above the number 294. The temple entrance doors and framing were transferred complete from the Register Square premises to the new location. The door gives on to a long hallway flanked by the stairs rising up one side and to the left is the dining room with its now U-shaped tables which thus accommodate the maximum number of people in what would otherwise be a modest dining area.

The stairs wind upwards to a landing with a preparation room to one side of the Temple entrance and you then quickly find yourself in the main room of the building. It is not overlarge, being about the dimensions of a double cube with walls covered with tall record boards—the lodge, Constitutional Chapter starting in 1794, Beverlac Mark Lodge beginning in 1881, St John of Beverley College SRIA and a number of others. The hall is the home of much masonry and it seems like it. Indeed the amazing sensation is that this hall has been in use for much more than the years of its actual operation. This is due to the possession of so many items that have much longer connections and the decor of the temple which is certainly reminiscent of mid-Victorian times.

The east end is the most marked as we must now expect. In the centre of a light crimson wall decorated with *fleur de lis* and hearts that reaches up to a pronounced gold and crimson dado we see a beautifully constructed circular arch of smooth ashlars with a superb keystone at the apex. From the keystone is suspended a replica of the seal design once given to Constitutional Lodge by R. M. Beverley, whilst emerging from behind the apex of the arch, in true Royal Arch style, is a blaze of golden circle and rays shining down upon the Master's chair and pedestal beneath. The apse wall on which this is painted is otherwise deep blue.

In the apse stands the austere but finely made Master's chair of oak, with two formal pillars and small globes as the back frame and a triangular headpiece bearing an upturned square. To left and right of the alcove are two other chairs with one a Bible and the other a full blazing sun in the headpiece, respectively for the chaplain on the Master's right and the IPM on his left. The chairs of the wardens are made to an identical design save that their headpieces carry a level and plumbline respectively. In regard to their pedestals the Master's is clearly smaller, older and made of walnut or mahogany whilst those of the other officers are of oak and have a much smaller base. That of the Senior Warden has a level on its front but the Junior Warden's has nothing.

What is of most interest at these places are the miniature columns cum candleholders which are set on shelves that protrude from the left-hand side of each pedestal. They were made in 1807 by Bro Montgomery of Constitutional Lodge. They are all identical in style with a base of steps in chequered design, a rectangular pediment, the column itself (fluted and with moulded top and bottom), a capital, a gilded sphere upon it, and the candleholder with blue candle thereon. Yet each is distinct in that the Junior Warden's column has seven base steps, the Senior Warden five and the Master only three. The pediments have a plumbline, a level, and a square in the same order and the spheres show delicate glass miniatures of a full orbed sun with rays, a crescent moon and the outline of a man's head and shoulders. These latter symbols refer, of course, to the words spoken by a Master after a candidate is restored to light and when he is shown for the first time the shape of the lodge.

What is even more fascinating in this hall, however, is that as in Sunderland, the Constitutional Lodge still possesses the ancient jewels of the Deacons that portray a sun and rays for the JD and a crescent moon and face for the SD. Indeed it is believed here that the Constitutional Lodge have always used these jewels for these officers, though the theory of these being first Wardens' jewels which were transferred to their 'deacons' when the former took over the level and the plumb-rule has been voiced.

(I would here refer the interested reader to the most exhaustive discussion of this whole matter in the Prestonian Lecture for 1985 by WBro Sinclair Bruce, a member of the Phoenix Lodge, Sunderland).

The visitor must by now have recognized the great character and sense of uniqueness of this Beverley Masonic Hall. Here, in a modest street, is captured a whole panorama of the local Freemasonry, kept alive by those who are only too aware of the many treasures that they have been entrusted with. By comparison with the work of the operative masons in the great Minster nearby it may seem but a little thing to the uninstructed eye but to us who know, or are daily learning to know, here is a hall that will stir memory and keep alive a necessary tradition. It is worth an hour's pause on your journey.

BOLTON

The Hall near t'owd Church

THERE IS A fascinating reference to ancient Bolton masonry in the records of Anchor and Hope Lodge No 37 which, since 1760, has held the distinguished position of being the Premier Lodge in Lancashire. It was constituted in 1732 and under the No 105 was noted as meeting in a 'Private Room' which is thought to have been in Churchgate opposite to the 'Man & Scythe Inn'. The extract from the history is as follows: 'The Brethren assembled in white gloves, with long cuffs or gauntlets and white leather aprons and at the making of a Mason the Brethren would strike their aprons with their hands three times which was to make a loud report, the Tyler parading an adjoining room to keep guard.'

What is fascinating is not simply the fact that masons a long way from Lancashire can still clearly recognise the scene and practices that were customary 255 years ago but that actual mementoes of these early days are still preserved in the present Freemasons Hall in Institute Street, Bolton. Not only are there samples of these leather aprons which were then normal attire but in the room used as a partial library and museum we have preserved a costume such as was worn by an 18th century Tyler along with the sword of his office. As you gaze at the large semi-circular black hat with its masonic emblems, the full-length heavy overcoat with its red cuffs and neck facings, its double row of gold buttons and gold edged cape, and the ivory-handled, curved cavalry-type sword one can all the more appreciate the dignity and importance attached by lodges to this essential officer. In the minutes of Lodge 37 we read for 1798: 'That the Tyler have a cloake and cap to keep him warm in cold weather.' The rig still preserved well fulfils that intention. It is worth pointing out that the Tyler was also provided thus because he was the messenger or postman who had to deliver the 'lawful summons' on behalf of the Master or Secretary and this was also why he was paid.

Yet it was 155 years after the founding of Anchor and Hope Lodge before the masons in Bolton could enjoy their own permanent lodging. Anchor and Hope members met successfully in the Hope Inn, the Boar's Head, the Legs of Man, the Four Horse Shoes, the Swan and even the Church Institute before 1887, and the Lodge of Antiquity, No 146, met in the Fox, the Crown, the Black Horse, the Weavers and many others. It is no surprise, therefore, that these two lodges were very much in support of the plan considered in 1879 for finding a suitable place for permanent residence but sadly they were alone in their determination and the discussions on this matter temporarily ceased.

During the next two years negotiations resumed over some premises in Bowker's Row where it was intended to rent accommodation at the Sales Room.

Unhappily the time taken in discussion and the low rent offered led to another tender being accepted from the Incorporated Law Society and thus the hope of finding a lasting home for Bolton masons was again deferred. In August 1886, however, a yet further attempt at a solution was made by appointing a Joint Committee of local lodges and on the 6th of that month a gathering of numerous brethren from many lodges unanimously agreed to rent premises in Silverwell Street, for the purpose of holding regular masonic meetings there. The proposed premises were to be constructed by Mr R. M. Thirlwind according to plans submitted by a Bro M. Robinson and a plan for furnishing and renting the finished building was also drawn up. Anchor and Hope Lodge was, not surprisingly, the first body to meet in the new centre on 5 September, 1887.

In the account given by the Reporter of the Bolton *Weekly Guardian* edition for Friday, 10 September, 1887 we read:

> A new building in Institute Street, off Silverwell Street, was formally opened to the Craft on Monday evening last, the Anchor and Hope Lodge No 37, of which G. P. Brockbank, P.G.Std.B.(Eng) is the Secretary, taking possession in a body. Congratulatory speeches were delivered and a vote of condolence was forwarded to the widow of Brother Rooke Pennington, an esteemed member of the

The earlier temple looking east. Behind the pedestal can be seen an array of four organs and the display of armorial banners.

Above: *The large lodge room at Bolton with the pillars in the west and kneeling chair between them.* Below: *Some early Knights Templar provincial priory jewels and an early Mark Master Mason's apron in the shape of a keystone.*

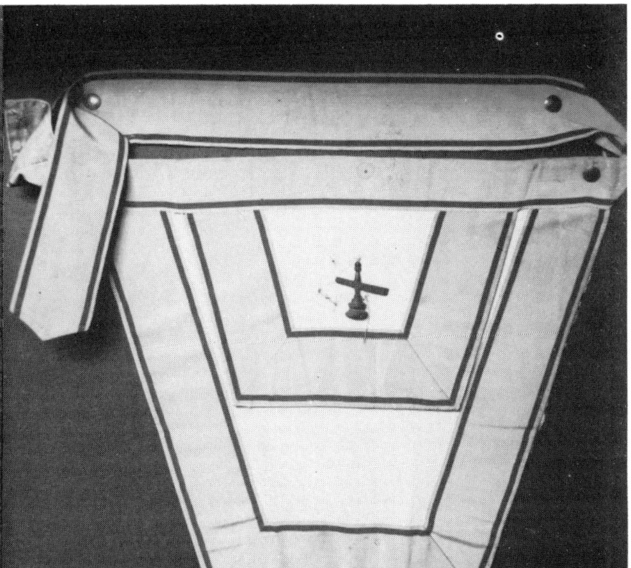

Brotherhood. There are over 200 members of the Craft in the Borough and the acquisition of this handsome building in a central yet quiet portion of the Town cannot fail to prove a great boon. The Hall is in every way adapted to the purpose for which it is set apart, whilst the furnishing has been carried out on a most elaborate scale, the walls being embellished with numerous old and valuable masonic relics, extending over a period of over 150 years. On the first floor is a roomy banquetting hall divided by revolving shutters from the Lodge Room of which the half religious and all mysterious air will awe the uninitiated and doubtless instruct the members of the Craft. On the ground floor are the Smoke Room, Library and Porter's Room and the lavatories. The upper part of the building is allotted to the caretaker and provision is made in the basement for storage.

On 28 September St George's Lodge No 1723 held its own first meeting in Institute Street. Although Bolton masons *always* refer to going to "Silverwell Street", meaning "The Hall", the hall was never in that street. Probably when the plans were being discussed there was no Institute Street. That only came about through the area being developed and Institute Street created. On the Ordnance Survey map of 1850 the area formed part of the gardens of Silverwell House. On this occasion the brethren were addressed by WBro G. Parker Brockbank, PM, PGStdBr, who had been a prime mover in the setting up of the new centre and who was also known locally as 'The Father of Freemasonry in Bolton'. He pointed out on this occasion that when the first of the present lodges was set up in Bolton in 1832 its meeting place had been no more than 100 yards from the place in which they were then assembled. He also expressed the hope that good fellowship would long exist amongst all the lodges meeting under the one roof, that no jealousies should prevail and that all would be animated by an earnest desire to promote in every possible way the best interests of the Craft. His words were apt for the time and would seem to have been fully taken to heart in all the years that have followed. The use, extension and general state of the Bolton Masonic Hall would seem to fully bear that out.

In 1908 an important stage in the life of the present hall took place when the Deed was drawn up between six representatives of the lodges meeting at the Freemasons Hall including one John Benjamin Goulburn, Accountant, (whose name is especially revered in East Lancashire) and four other persons (including a Margaret Alice Thirlwind) whereby the Trusteeship of these premises passed into the care of wholly masonic trustees and from that time onwards the care of what is now the Hall in Institute Street passed into the hands of the brethren themselves. It is a charge that has been handsomely borne for in October 1928 the Rt Hon The Earl of Derby, PGM, assisted by Grand Provincial Grand Officers, attended to preside over the dedication of the additional premises that were now to house the many more lodges that wished to join their older predecessors there. As you approach the building to-day you can see the two fine doorways that mark the first and second stages of the structure. The older entrance has more of the embellishments of an earlier period with its formal arch and keystone over the leaded fanlight and a richly carved pediment with masonic emblems beneath a still higher arch. The second door has all the appearance of a lesser version of the other Freemasons' Hall in Great Queen Street, London, and now rightly forms the principal entry to the premises.

In 1978 the Rt Hon Lord Hewlett, PGM, carried out a further ceremony when he inaugurated the Social Club Room which was created from some of the space left free by the use of the newer Temples and ancillary rooms that are now situated in the 'new extension' of 1928. The result is that Bolton masons now have an extremely well-appointed recreational area in addition to all the other fine appointments for their purely Masonic ceremonial activities. It means in a very real sense that Bolton masons today have used to the full the opportunities given to them by an earlier generation and have retained some of their fine history and traditions whilst also making this hall a very acceptable meeting place for modern masons and their wives. It is not every major masonic hall that can offer a Snug, lunch-time snacks, a maple dance floor, an aluminium ceiling with many thousands of leaves and an impressive array of comfortable hide and mahogany Captains Chairs. 'Anchor and Hope' or 'Antiquity' members of 200 years ago would indeed be envious if they could see what their present successors enjoyed.

They too, however, have left their mark on the much larger and more substantial building that we see today. Pass, if you will, through the social club area to the oldest part of the site and you will enter the original temple. It has many marks of being a typical Victorian structure with its simple plaster walls, a lower course of plain board panelling all around the room, its ecclesiastical-style white timbered roof and gabled ceiling in crimson with brown edging, its surviving gas brackets and solid oak chairs or green leather seating around the four sides of a richly woven red carpet patterned with cream roses. To add to the dating of the hall the main feature, behind the WM's place on a red plush dais, is what looks at first glance like a sideboard with a large Portrait on it of WBro Thos. Sharples Barlow, a well-respected Bolton mason and benefactor and later PGM of the Mark Degree. It is in fact an American organ of substantial proportions and looking in good order though not now used. It is flanked by two other organ consoles, one of them possibly Edwardian vintage and in black oak, and the other the modern electronic instrument. Together with four fine larger armchairs for the principal officers in the east, themselves of early or mid-Victorian craftmanship,

Left: *Complete Tyler's uniform used for delivering summonses in the town.* Right: *18th century Master's jewel.*

the total effect is a fine replica of what a meeting place for Freemasonry in Bolton must have looked like when this hall was originally acquired.

Yet there is another feature of this room that makes it specially memorable. Above the items in the east just mentioned there hangs a fine array of Banners with very distinctive armorial bearings. The banners themselves are clearly from an ealier period and there must be many who came into this, the 'Chapter Room' as it is usually known, who may wonder, as does any enquiring visitor, how these banners came to be placed here and to whom they belonged. The information concerning them is provided, not unfittingly in view of the first name of the street in which this Hall stood, by a member of Silverwell Lodge, WBro Philip Haworth.

The actual designs on display today are found in a book, presented by WBro George Barnes to the then Secretary of the Hall Committee, Bro J. T. Hill, and entitled 'This book of original designs for Lodge Banners'. The book contained 67 pages, each with a banner design and all done by one who was obviously an excellent craftsman. Of the 67 designs only two are not 'personal' banners: the two are those of Anchor and Hope Lodge and St Peter's Rose Croix, Chapter No 31, whilst the remainder refer to family names. The presenter of the book was the proprietor of a printing business (Hasler Watson and Co) which is no longer in business in the town.

There are alternative suggestions as to whom the banners relate. One opinion has it that they recalled masters of Anchor and Hope Lodge only, whilst another view is that they referred to Masters of many lodges that used the building up to 1903. It is impossible here to list the whole of the names that have been researched but a few will show the wide range of East Lancashire families involved—le Gendre, Starkie, Lever, Horrocks, Heywood, Crompton, Tong, Lathom and Brockbank. Indeed it appears that the fashion for banners could well be laid at the door of that brother to whom reference has already been made, George Parker Brockbank. Born in 1826 he died in 1888 after realising his one great ambition which was to see all the Bolton lodges housed in one building. In his tireless efforts to enhance the beauty and dignity of their new masonic home the banners would have been, as they still are, a special and distinctive feature. Their being placed there under his direction shows that they are already over a century old, and that they do derive from that era seems proven by two other facts.

One is that when in its peregrinations the Anchor and Hope lodge moved from the Church Institute to an earlier home at the Swan Hotel it is recorded that Bros J. Newton and G. P. Brockbank were responsible for laying out the masonic room which was described as 'being beautifully fitted out with a number of masonic banners and also Masonic jewels . . .' It seems likely that what was customary in temporary accommodation was also followed when a more permanent home was established. Furthermore, on being a Founder of St George's No 1723, Bro Brockbank not only put up his banner there but persuaded his successors to do the same, at least until the time when that lodge transferred to the new hall, and some years afterwards. The fact that in addition to being presented with a PM's jewel past occupants of the Chair in that lodge and some of the others each had an additional enamel replica of their family crest added to the ribbon confirms that the designs were readily available for the banner practice.

Before we leave this room and its connections with the past it is worth noting that nowadays it is used hardly at all for Craft ceremonies and is generally reserved for the Royal Arch and other additional degree meetings. In Bolton this is another strong link with the past for in the history of the RA Chapter of Concord attached to the Anchor and Hope lodge it is stated that down to August, 1833, all meetings were termed "A General Encampment" and in this very month a minute states 'Royal Arch encampment of Super excellent Masons'. It continues 'The members assembled at 2 pm, opened the craft lodge, 3 Brethren were passed the Chair, and the lodge was closed. The Chapter was opened at ½ past 4 o'clock and 6 candidates were exalted to the degree of Excellent Super-Excellent Holy Royal Arch Masons. At ½ past 6-0, 49 companions sat down to a cold dinner. . . .'

In addition to these apparently 'exotic' practices there are other records in local minutes books showing that the Ark, Mark, Link and Wrestle degrees were conferred in 1832 and the Knight Templar from 1785 to 1789, and again in 1834, 1841 and 1843. It should not surprise the briefed visitor to remark near the doorway of the old hall a peculiar stone which 'was brought from Jerusalem by Sir John Fletcher in May 1869. It was the Quoin stone in the doorway of the Hospital Chapter (at present in ruins) built by the Knights Templars, situate near the Church of the Holy Sepulchre xxxxxxx

Presented to St. James of Jerusalem Encampment, Bolton . . . June 30, AL 5824, AD 1820. AO 752. . . .'

The archives room and museum in the main part of the building has a wonderful array of treasures of no less interest. Here we find some most distinctive Victorian KT Provincial jewels with a Maltese Cross in red enamel and a white circular centrepiece indicating the office conferred, and, from even earlier still, a most carefully preserved and copper plate handwritten certificate for 'our well beloved Brother and Trusty Companion THOMAS LEDWARD'. Considering the date of its issue, and that being at a time when Christian masonry was generally considered to have been 'in the doldrums', it is worth recording in full:

> Having passed through the different Degrees of Craft and Holy Royal Arch Masonry and having Shewd himself worthy by his great Zeal and Perserverance through the amazing Trials made of his Faith and Valour which he justly sustained and honourably maintained, did duly Obtain and was by Us admitted and Dubbed a Sir Knight Companion of the Most Religious and Military Order of Knights Templars, in our encampment at Manchester, upon the 29th day of April in the year of our Blessed Redeemer, 1830, and subsequently admitted a Knight of the Red Cross, and of the Order of Malta . . .

The certificate, which has 5 definite signs at the top relative to the degrees mentioned (and it is instructive to see them described as degrees *after* the Union), is signed by the candidate and countersigned on the authority of the late Thos. Dunckerley from 1799.

Alongside this very precious document is another showing how Sir Knight Stephen Blair in 1849, AL 1853, AO 731, was duly admitted to the Conclave and Chapter of St James of Jerusalem held 'in their Field of Encampment, Bolton, and thus acknowledged a Knight of the Religious and Military order of HRDM Grand Elected Masonic Knights Templars KDOSH of St John of Jerusalem & Palestine Etc. Etc. Etc.' Yet again we can see displayed, from one of the books here, 2 tracing boards and an altar layout of the A and A Rite such as few would be familiar with at present.

The range is very wide. On the walls is a framed certificate of 13 November 1873 which is addressed to all St Lawrence masons stating that Alfred Wareing has been regularly Accepted and Admitted to that degree alone in Rochdale; whilst in a book from the library we read that two Bolton masons (Bros Thomas Entwisle and G. P. Brockbank) are to be elected as members of the Metropolitan Lodge of the Order of St Lawrence at Red Lion Square, Holborn in 1879. It can thus be seen that Bro Brockbank was not merely a 'local masonic enthusiast'. Indeed there is a file kept by GPB containing circulars/summons of the lodges he had visited—America—Middle East and Far East.

In a Province that has so highly regarded the Mark degree it is not surprising to find distinctive items here. One is an apron in the shape of a keystone with a crossed mallet and chisel on its similarly keystone-shaped flap and the pale blue colour having faded between its red borders. Close by, on the wall, we have an 1865 Mark certificate which is unusual in that it shows not merely an elongated keystone in perspective at its centre, with differing 'marks' in the two circles of letters flanking it, but the whole is issued by St John's, Bolton No 2 'Held under Warrant from the Supreme Grand Royal Arch Chapter of Scotland'. Thus is retained a visible link with an unhappy stage in the progress of English Mark masonry. (It is also worth noting that several collar jewels of the same St John's Mark Lodge TI in Bolton indicate that it was so originally warranted and the Inner Guard's jewel is unique in the land for it carries the letters TK which apparently mean 'Time Keeper', though why that is so no-one really knows.)

For the Royal Arch student there is a fascinating set of breast jewels of very varied designs but three in particular of the Pillars and Arch style which one sees elsewhere but here made into exceptional pieces by having three gilt crowns above the Arch. They are clearly a set for the Principals at the time when headdress was still usual and they are properly prized here as being in such pristine condition. Close to this case there is also a most beautifully framed Royal Arch certificate for 1828, showing a broken arch with the faced sun pouring down its light through the gap of a keystone and within the arch two cherubic faces with wings in a cloudy canopy. The wording across the top of the certificate is also unexpected: "The Second Lancashire Union Band" and between the two Corinthian Pillars that support the arch are two descending rows of figures with aprons with the following virtues upon them:

Wisdom	Truth
Strength	Light
Beauty	Power

whilst on the chequered pavement below stands yet another aproned figure holding out his left hand like the others. The chapter ribbon on the left of the document has a large well-preserved seal.

The Craft has its own special items—a 'First Angel' certificate of the Antients Grand Lodge dated 1880 and showing Faith, Hope and Charity: on or by the three pillars, a pair of highly coloured French prisoner of war jewels in circular gold cases: a most impressive Master's gilt jewel showing the sun with a face and its rays between a highly ornamented pair of compasses extended on a segment of a circular rule and the whole intertwined with a flowing tasselled metal ribbon. Even this piece, however, is eclipsed by the private jewel of Peter Ainsworth, a whitster of Halliwell, who was initiated into Anchor and Hope lodge on 27 April, 1765 and whose delicately carved gilt adornment is reputed to be 'the oldest private jewel in existence'. It was discovered amongst the silver at Smithills Hall when it was purchased by the Corporation in 1939 and handed back to this lodge by Thomas Profit WM. Even a Sketchley token of 1790 and a most unusual glass collecting box that was illuminated when used by St John's Lodge 436 in the early nineteenth-century pale into comparative insignificance. We are in the presence of a true antiquity.

To emphasise that ancient ancestry one cannot fail to mention the most precious treasure that this hall possesses. It is a copy of the etched minutes of the Grand Lodge Quarterly Communication of 21 November, 1732. It is unique in the most literal sense of the word as it is the only known copy to exist. It is printed on paper, alas much mutilated, from a copper plate engraved by Pine. It was the practice up to that time to print off copies in the presence of the Grand Secretary and, when the necessary number had been produced, to bring the plates to the Grand Master

The smaller temple at Bolton has two superb globes positioned on the west edge of the chequered floorcovering.

or his Deputy who saw the plates destroyed. The Minutes of the above Communications were the last to be so etched for all subsequent ones were printed in letterpress. Not that Bolton could be allowed to have just a one-off even here for as well as this precious document there is also a letter in the handwriting of the Grand Secretary, Will Reid, to Edward Entwistle in the year that he founded Anchor and Hope Lodge in 1732.

Before we part from this truly memorable haven of ancient Freemasonry, close by its even more ancient Parish Church, we should not fail to re-enter the newer extension of the present hall and tour the main temples that are used by Craft masons today. Here is the very best of craftsmanship and a set of masonic rooms that would do honour to any centre. Rising from the spacious entrance hall with its dignified mahogany panelling we climb a spacious staircase with its leaded landing windows and come to the rich entrance doors of the main temple. Within we see a sumptuous and stately room with a gently curved roof picked out in pale blue and cream. The lower walls are again panelled throughout and fine leather-upholstered chairs surround the pale blue carpet with its chequered centrepiece in tiles. At the western end of the chequered floor stand two lofty wooden pillars with simulated nets and pomegranates at their heads and above them two beautiful globes, the kneeling stool between them. The pedestals and the principal officers' chairs are of equal quality and, though perhaps not of an antiquity mentioned elsewhere in this book, are already showing the effects of polish and patina. One open-backed and armed chair belonging to 'Antiquity' dates from about 1776 and it sits well among six other handsome Chippendales. A heavier straightbacked chair in the 'Chapter Room' belongs to St John's Lodge, now No 221.

In the adjoining and slightly smaller temple on the floor below the same quality of workmanship is retained and at the end of the chequered floor in this case are two normal globes of seventeenth century style on their graceful tripods. The placing of ashlars at their older positions in the northern and southern corners of the flooring will strike those who are not familiar with such a practice.

As we pause before our departure from this memorable Masonic Hall in East Lancashire it might be worthwhile to recall that William Howarth wrote in the history of St John's Lodge here on the occasion of its 150th anniversary in 1965.

'Alexander Pope wrote "The proper study of mankind is man". This is a single facet of it. A looking back and a looking forward should help us better to know ourselves.'

I am certain that as we enter these portals and see what the past has offered and what the future can maintain we can only be better men and masons.

BRADFORD

The Connaught Rooms of West Yorkshire

No-one can pretend that Bradford today is quite what it was a decade ago. To walk in its streets is to notice the difference. This is equally true of the hall in Manningham Lane to which I would now introduce the reader. Indeed it has to be admitted that visiting an antiquarian bookshop just a few doors away in recent years I was unaware that close by was one of the most remarkable masonic complexes in the North of England. I should have known if I had but lifted my eyes to see the front canopy over the street. It says plainly: 'Connaught Rooms'.

The building is an impressive one despite its present rather run-down exterior. It is four storeys high and occupies a substantial island site between two local streets. The depth of the building is about twice its breadth and, as we shall see, it was planned on an imposing scale. The lodges that were to support it from its opening came here from the Masonic Hall, Westgate which had been occupied in 1922, following the use before that of several smaller premises. It was built on the site of a Doctor's residence and must have seemed a veritable Masonic 'palace', emphasising the important place of Freemasonry in this area in the 1920s. Today the hall is managed by the Bradford Masonic Association and it was by the permission of that body that I was able to see the glories of an age that is past.

People still enter by that same majestic entrance under the front canopy and find themselves in the ground floor foyer.

On the left, and beneath five fine stained-glass windows, are two stones. One speaks for itself:

'This founders' stone was laid by RWorBro Viscount Lascelles, KG, DSO. Provincial Grand Master of West Yorkshire on 2 November 1926.'

On the other stone are inscribed the names of the lodges that shared in helping to make the erection of this new Masonic Hall possible: Harmony 600, Shakespeare 1018, Eccleshill 1034, Prince of Wales 1648, Acacia 2321, Victoria 2669, Ionic 3210, King Edward VII 3442, Corinthian 3600, Peace 3988, Doric 4073, Faith 4223 and Temple 4963.

It can thus be seen that from the very start this hall was meant to serve a substantial body of local masons and there have been countless consecrations of new lodges since the day that the original 13 looked forward to occupying the site. When to the Craft lodges, as we are reminded by the emblems in the upstairs leaded lights, we add the Mark, Royal Arch, Rose Croix and Knight Templar bodies that were to meet here the visitor can begin to grasp the size of the population that it was planned to accommodate. Moreover it was intended that not only would these units each have satisfactory locations for their usual ceremonies and dining but there would also be ample provision for their social and recreational periods as well. In addition a visit to the now vacated and desolate basement area shows you (as we see still in the Manchester Temple) the arrangement of 5 separate rehearsal rooms for the lodges, containing pictures relevant to each individual unit, with space in the corridors for their hats, coats, regalia, pottery and lodge furniture. The space was planned on a most generous scale and those who first occupied the building must have been most grateful for a practice of the Craft that was both adequate and memorable. 50 years later it was also to prove very costly.

To return to the foyer, however, we must pause and look in more detail at the stained glass windows which were mentioned. Starting from the left they display the following features:

A. Below a sign of the Royal Arch (the shapes on the top of the altar) is a scene showing a man cutting down trees (is it Noah?). Under this forest picture with its rich colours are the words, 'Presented by the Lodge of Harmony and its daughter lodges and unveiled by H. Charles Slaite P.G.M. October 31, 1955'.

B. At the top of this window is a level and the picture below shows Solomon and Hiram Abiff holding a level and beneath this scene the dates 1928–1953,

Lodge of Harmony furniture with the secretary's desk adjacent to the Worshipful Master's pedestal.

September 29th. (These refer to the fact that the window was placed there on the same day in 1953 as the Hall was consecrated in 1928).

C. Under the square and compasses in the position for a F.C. there is a most richly coloured Solomon holding the temple before him on his crooked arms. Below him at the two sides of the window are 2 owls (representing Wisdom) and below them the words, 'In memory of Henry Emerson Bower' with the name flanked by 'Initiated 1905' and 'Died 1943'.

D. The Plumbline crowns this window with a picture of Hiram Abiff holding a drawing or plan below the words and underneath that figure the name 'Edward Smith, Chairman'. These words, like the emblem and figure above, are flanked by the designs or letters showing this brother's achievements—JGD, OBE and Mark Grand rank (on the left) and Grand Chapter, Provincial Prior and King Edward VII (on the right).

E. The last window shows a PM's jewel above the picture of a quarryman and underneath this the words, 'Unveiled by Clifford Smith on 31 October, 1955'. Around the edges of this window are emblems of the other 12 lodges that first occupied this hall.

After such a colourful and dedicated introduction for the newcomer it will not surprise the visitor to pass halfway down the panelled foyer and pause to push

The Treasurer's desk is next to the Junior Warden's pedestal.

open two fine oak doors to gaze upon the hall's own enormous ballroom. It was built to accommodate 350 persons and has its own gallery for the attending musicians. It stretches up to the floor of the third storey and it was, of course, able to meet the needs of a vast dining party should there be a call for this from the Province. It still has one of the finest sprung floors in the whole of the country and the chandeliers must have made a magnificent effect when the hall was the scene of a Ladies Evening or Ball. You can well believe that in its heyday this was a focal point of the City's social events for the ballroom and main dining room were always available for outside public functions if they were not required by members of the Craft. The result is that the Connaught Rooms in Bradford have been known locally at least as well as their namesake in the London scene. Opposite the ballroom is the oakroom, a retiring room for those who might not wish to dance but preferred to sit, chat or smoke.

Joining all the floors, and in addition to the marble staircase, were two sets of lifts: one for the use of lodge members and one for the servicing of the hall in the rear. These lifts are now somewhat out of date and the Association is faced with a colossal bill if they are to be brought up to modern standards of safety and design. Climbing up to the second storey you discover a most attractive and prestigious vestibule or landing surrounded by marble walls, large portraits, and another set of tall stained glass windows.

The portraits include the Earl of Mexborough, at one time Provincial Grand Master, Sir Anthony Gadie, Lord Mayor of Bradford and also another PGM, and Sir Henry Whitehead, renowned locally as the main benefactor behind the provision of these premises (though in fact his promised contribution was never quite what had been anticipated and had to be made up by extreme efforts on the part of the first occupants of the hall). The windows were the gift of Mr E. Everard Gates in memory of his father, Bro Ernest H. Gates, in April 1930 and they portray in a restrained and dignified fashion the activities that have constantly involved those who have attended here as masons. From left to right, as you face them from inside, the windows display at the top the emblems of

Rose Croix: Knight Templar: Royal Arch: Mark: Craft:

and between them and the Virtues spelt out below each order there are symbolic figures representing

Truth: Faith: Hope: Charity: Brotherly Love:

The glass was set in place in 1930 and has thus adorned this heart of the hall for almost the whole period of its existence.

To the right of the windows and along the wall at right angles to them is a large piece of Italian furniture called a Credenza. It contains several unsorted and assorted items of masonic interest and it is the intention of the Association to have this mini-museum transferred to the floor above where the lodges normally meet so that there can be renewed interest by brethren in some of the hall's lodges' more ancient past. Opposite this display cabinet you pass through the large double doors into the main dining room with its attractive and deeply coffered plaster ceiling. This room could take 250 persons for dinner and was obviously a perfect addition to the ballroom on the floor below. The dining room even has its own organ and the room was actually used for Installation meetings of the larger lodges when the members and their guests could not easily fit into the rooms above. The room is enhanced by a huge wall-painting, a canvas which represents Drake's Ransom of San Domingo, and which must have formed a fine backcloth to the merriment and festivity of gatherings in this salon.

Across the vestibule you pass down a small corridor to the back of the gallery for the ballroom below thus revealing how the musicians could enter and retire without disturbing the dancers on the floor. In addition each floor is provided with an efficient food lift system so that hot food could be supplied direct from the kitchens on the top floor to each of the suites on the floors below. On the second storey there was an additional dining room as well as the main hall so that all those attending any dance or social function could be served, or two lodges could be served simultaneously.

Yet the most interesting room on this floor was what is now a small practice room to the left of the stained glass windows. Its fascination for the student of the Craft is that here are preserved the three officers' chairs from the Lodge of Harmony No 600 warranted in 1852. They are well-made, attractive items of mid-Victorian vintage, with pillared arms and legs, and backs pleasantly decorated with the emblems for Master and Wardens at their head. Looking at them you begin to savour something of an older Yorkshire masonry than is revealed elsewhere. There are also several samples of the 84 circular-backed chairs which were also produced for the seating in lodge at that same period and with the distinctive, inlaid Treasurer's pedestal and the 3, 2 and 1 stepped chequered plinths for the principal officers' chairs you really do take a step back in time as you stand in this small room. Here, you feel, is part of Bradford's heritage and a share of it that ought not to be lost.

Stained glass window depicting the various degrees worked at Bradford hall.

Mounting once more to the third storey we find an excellent arrangement of lodge rooms and dining areas so placed that each lodge can have space to itself and be separate from any other group meeting in the building at the same time. The furnishings in the lodge rooms are of the best quality for the 1920s and it is because the lodge furniture in each case is built into the whole décor of the rooms that we see why the furniture from the past was no longer required for official meetings. The dining areas are commodious and attractive but the illuminated panel in the York Lodge Room is an especially striking feature. Service to these rooms is handy and unobtrusive from the service lift unit and the Association is satisfied that they can now provide a more than effective answer to the needs of the lodges that remain.

For as you move upstairs yet again, to what was once the ample living quarters for the hall manager (including a large roof garden area) and is still the modern kitchen complex, you begin to realise that there is a significant difference between the ground and first floors and the space above. The Secretary of the Association explained the situation. Whereas the rooms began with 13 lodges which soon became 18 and to those were added 10 chapters, conclaves and Mark or Royal Ark Mariner lodges the sheer cost of maintaining this huge plant had begun during the last decade to become a burden which some freemasons from the outer parts of the city could no longer face.

New and smaller lodge rooms were built or rented around the area and today the Connaught Rooms serve only 10 Craft lodges and 7 units of the other degrees. To save money it was recently decided to shut off the first two floors for masonic use and thus save some £17,000 in rates. When it is realised that the rooms only cost £90,000 to build and are insured for a present re-instatement value of £4.8m it can be appreciated that trying to maintain such a vast complex is taxing the efforts of those who have continued to meet here. The problems of trying to let the lower floors, which were so tailor-made for masonic purposes and are such a tribute to Bradford's masonic past, is far from easy, especially in the economic climate of the area today. To repair, maintain or adapt the building requires financial courage of a tall order. Yet the Masonic Association, with one elected member from each of the participating lodges and 10 coopted members plus the Master in office of each lodge, is determined to do what it can to save this truly memorable and magnificent hall from extinction. It is not only a monument to the past: it is a base from which some masons can confidently look to the future. I for one will never pass it again without acknowledging the 'Connaught Rooms' of the North.

Entrance hall stained glass windows.

CARLISLE

The Hall in the Terrace of Fisher Street

JUST AS WE have elsewhere found ourselves in the interesting hall on the border at Berwick-upon-Tweed so we also need to make a visit to the other end of the border at Carlisle. Masonry in these parts is sufficiently ancient, for there is a mention of a lodge constituted in Carlisle in 1766, which was meeting at the Black Bull Inn, in Annetwell Street, in 1783, though that was also the year in which it was erased.

Before that sad event, however, we read that in 1772, and on St John's Day, the lodge received a deputation from Lochmaben and the brethren 'went to Church and heard sermon from the Revd Brother Andrew Jeffries, Minister of the Gospel at Ruthwell, a Member of this Lodge.' The same link with Scots brethren was evident in the life of Harmony Lodge, founded here in 1771, and lasting up to the decease of that lodge in 1851.

Yet the strongest connection across the border was to emerge in the life of Carlisle's third lodge, Union No 216, when in 1785, and to quote the lodge historian, RA Clarke, 'a number of Scotsmen—Brethren of Lodge St Andrew, Annan—came to the city, not in a hostile manner like the Ephraimites who crossed the River Jordan in Jephtha's day, but on a peaceful mission' and 'applied to their Grand Lodge in Edinburgh for permission to hold a lodge in Carlisle, to be called the Union Lodge'. Its number was to be 216.

That precious Charter of Dispensation is still a prized possession of the hall in Carlisle and two parts of it are worth recording: it is the response to a presentation by those who 'are all Master masons residing in the City of Carlyle(*sic*), Praying the Grand Lodge of Scotland aforesaid to erect them into a Regular Body or Lodge under the title and designation of "the Union Carlyle Lodge" with all the usual powers Together with an ample certificate . . .'. It continues: 'And all Regular Lodges holding of the Grand Lodge of Scotland are in the meantime hereby required to own and respect the Brethren aforesaid in the same way and manner as if they were erected into a Regular Lodge'. It is no less fascinating to learn that this unique and valuable document was presented to the lodge in September 1906 by Bro James Baty, PM acting on behalf of WBro T. J. Armstrong of Newcastle upon Tyne.

They so worked for 11 years until, on 30 July, 1796, A Charter or Warrant was granted from the Grand Lodge of England under which the present Union Lodge, now numbered 310, began its existence. It is worth recording that members of the new Union Lodge nevertheless kept up their links with Annan and when the Lodge Annan St Andrew's held its centenary in 1860 there is recorded a deputation of six members fron Union, Carlisle. This connection continued until the Annan lodge finally closed in 1885.

The place of meeting for this 'English' Union Lodge was named in the Warrant as being the Grapes Inn at Carlisle, which was actually no 1, English Street—a surely appropriate address. Yet even this was not always apparently adequate for their local practice for in 1796, on the festival of St John (26 December) we are told that 'this lodge joined in procession with the Lodge of Harmony and proceeded to the Cathedral, where an excellent sermon was preached by Bro Pattinson. And then returned to Mrs Pringle's and dined, where we spent the evening, being visited by several of the brethren of the Lodge of Harmony, the lodges of Annan, Langholm and Penrith.' By the 11th of January they had moved to Mrs Elliot's, the Pack Horse Inn—but still in English Street.

It is again on the walls of the present Masonic Hall that we read a little more of the Union Lodge's history. By 1817 the lodge was giving Certificates of Membership and one of these is herewith reproduced.

Lodge of Union Carlisle, 579
Meeting at Miss Johnson's, King's Head Inn,
Fisher Street.

These are to certify that Brother John Nixon, of Brampton, was, at the age of forty years, regularly and duly initiated into the mysteries of Masonry in this lodge on Thursday, the 25th day of January, 1814, that he was passed on the 28th day of February, 1815, and raised on the 28th day of February, 1815, and having found him to be a worthy Brother we recommend him as such to all Masons and Lodges to be received after due examination.

To this Certificate the said Brother John Nixon has in our presence signed his name at full length in the margin.

(There then follow the WM, SW, JW and Secretary's names)
Against the lodge seal it says 1817 AD 5817 AL

We have already seen how mutually the lodge was able to involve the church in its activities, or vice versa, and in 1823 the foundation stone of the Chapel of the prison at Carlisle was laid with masonic ceremonial by Brother Blamire, the Provincial Grand Master himself. It is a period of which the visitor to the hall at Carlisle is again reminded when he sees the ram's horn snuff 'mull' in the china cupboard for this was given to the Union Lodge by the departing Dumfries operative masons who had also come across to work on the building of the local gaol. It is not now used, but it was previously and figured regularly on the festive board. Its rollers show that it was easily sent down the table.

This connection with the church has persisted over the last century and quite apart from the Lord Bishop of Carlisle and the Dean of the Cathedral being in attendance when the PGM laid the foundation stone of the Cumberland Infirmary (1830) the visitor to today's Masonic Hall is bound to notice a framed document mentioning the Dedication of the Choir Paving at the Cathedral in 1933, which was given by local masons. The service form for the occasion is also preserved as one of the hall's decorations.

Mention has already been made of the china cupboard and at the Installation meeting on 27 December, 1832 thanks were expressed to Brothers Scott and Johnson for their handsome gift of 43 jugs which thus enabled each brother to take one home for his own use. There are now 28 of them intact in the lodge's possession and as that into which a brother's liquor was poured they give us today yet another insight into an earlier form of after-proceedings. When to these you add the larger jugs from which they were doubtless replenished (four of these having faces and one showing the earlier Victorian forms of Faith, Hope and Charity) and three examples of the engraved Union rummers that bore spirits, the delicately painted and inscribed punch bowls or the two slender candlesticks and the inlaid level (with square and compasses, sun, moon and alms-bags) that probably made the Master's centre piece at table, you realise that this hall is firmly preserving facets of past lodge practice that ought never to be lost. The tiny maul, bell and miniature silver 'dining' jewels for use by the WM, S and JW, Sec and DC also need mention.

The portrait of a previous Deputy Provincial Grand Master Bro Iredale also belongs to the hall and in July 1846 this brother was attended by numerous Union brethren to lay the foundation stone of St Kentigern's church at Aspatria 'by desire of the Right Revd the Lord Bishop' of the diocese. It was at last in July 1860 that a Lodge of Emergency was summoned to consider 'the desirability of removing the Lodge to private premises instead of holding it in a licensed house, with a view to promoting greater interest on the part of the members . . . ' (Clarke p.49). By October the first meeting took place in Barwise Court but alas the cost of

Carlisle Masonic Temple looking east.

altering and furnishing these rooms was so great that no banquet was able to be held at the Installation that year!

It was during their sojourn at this first real 'home' that Union Lodge procured its present fine tracing boards. They were painted by Bro Matthew Fisher, an artist who became Asst Secretary of the lodge on 26 March, 1861, and Secretary the year after—which fact is recorded with the 1862 Master's name at the foot and head of the Second Degree board. This second degree board is not too distinct from many others of the same period but it is remarkably clear in all its details and in its colour is exquisite. The name of the Deity is indicated by the Letter "G" at the top centre of the board and not over the middle Chamber entrance and there are three distinct chambers shown—a lower, middle and upper. There are indeed 15 steps from the ground to the middle landing.

The two fine globes of the terrestrial and celestial spheres, which are currently placed at the foot of the steps leading up to the WM's throne, were purchased in 1863 for the sum of one guinea. Their value today would be at least a thousand times that sum.

The first lodge meeting in yet further new 'private' rooms in Castle Street (17 January, 1866) saw the Rev William Cockett installed as Master. Whether or not he referred to it in his inaugural speech the new Master must have been delighted to know that it was from these very premises that Sir Walter Scott was married on 24 December, 1797. Certainly he would have been very impressed by the situation in which he found himself—upon a tall and dignified mahogany Master's Chair that has a fine padded back, with a curved headpiece carved and inscribed 'Union Lodge 589—William Moore—WM 1824' with a square and compass motif in the centre.

The chair's setting is also most impressive against a classical backdrop on the east wall, with two large pilasters flanking the chair and a triangular pediment supported on the cornice above them.

It was in 1895 that a joint committee of the Union and Bective lodges—the latter founded in April, 1875—discussed and agreed to purchase the premises in Fisher Street belonging to Mr Thomas Smithson. The cost was £950. A limited liability company was formed and the necessary alterations were made to suit the two lodges concerned. The builder was Robert Little, a member of the Union Lodge. The opening of the new premises was carried out in a most unusual manner by having the two lodges join in a united meeting in which the Union Lodge officers rehearsed the opening of the lodge in the three degrees, and the Bective officers then took over to do the closing ones.

The year 1915 saw the premises yet further developed so that they became what the visitor sees today. It is not a noticeable hall from the outside being but a natural frontage amongst the normal terrace of detached houses in what was one of Carlisle's better Victorian inner suburbs. The entrance hall might well be that of any prosperous mid-Victorian family and the decoration and furnishings have well retained the sense of the hall's original purpose. A large dining room to the rear is a natural addition to the premises but in no way affects the unity of the rest of the house. It is here that one sees the china cupboard mentioned earlier.

One mounts the stairs which are spacious and well graded to discover a separate robing room on the landing and two committee rooms beside the temple proper.

As with so many rooms that we see in this volume the surprise that one feels on entering these rooms for our ceremonies is heightened by the comparatively ordinary settings in which they appear. Here again, one enters a room in which immediately there are features to record that are too many to take in at once. Some of them have already been described in this history of Union Lodge but to see the east end in the context of the whole can also be a more memorable experience. The wide kneeling stool in front of the Senior Warden's pedestal, the large tripod and hanging ashlar immediately before it, the pleasantly carved screen in the very centre of the floor carrying the lodge's ancient warrant (already quoted from) and then the globes before the Master's place. At once the character and history of the lodge comes newly alive especially as there are other attendant features to fill out the whole.

Turning about one can see the interesting masonic clock that is fixed above the main entrance on the inner side. We have seen others (consider the one in Worksop) but in days when clocks of a much more humdrum nature adorn so many temple walls to see this is an added delight. Equally the old Union Lodge banner with its premier Grand Lodge arms impaled with those of the City of Carlisle has been well preserved and its dating reminds us of 160 years of Masonic life here—1796–1956. One might also notice the distinctive ballot box on the Secretary's table—foursquare and with a protruding central knob for its conveyance it bears the words FOR and AGAINST on two raised slits to left and right, but at the centre a smooth medallion of wood bearing the words, "Be just and fear not".

Away in the south west corner of the room is yet another delight—a pipe organ with a magnificent carved frame of classical style. On the left hand pillar is a top panel showing the sun in glory with a carved open volume of the sacred law beneath it, whilst on the right the top panel shows the moon and seven stars with a whole host of masonic tools and symbols running down the whole length of the pillar beneath. It must prove a most pleasing sight as well as being the source of that harmony which makes any ceremony that much more meaningful.

Anyone who comes to this modest but memorable outpost of our northern Freemasonry will be glad to know that the masons of this city have at last found here a home to be proud of. We have seen the tracing boards that spoke of Martin Fisher's care for his lodge and we can well close with a verse which was part of some lines written by him on the fly-leaf of the minute book which he began as Secretary in 1864—he wrote:

May the records herein by me traced
Still be of Unity and Love
Let us faithfully serve our Master here
And meet in the Grand Lodge above.

DURHAM

The Treasure of Old Elvet

FREEMASONRY IN DURHAM City has had a long and honourable history. The oldest lodge, or only surviving one, operating in 1870 is recorded as having held meetings in the Bird and Bush Inn in 1738. By 1763, when the lodge received its charter from the premier Grand Lodge, it was still meeting in an inn, the Marquis of Granby , in Sadler Street. This may well have been the original inn but renamed in honour of the British General of the Seven Years War, John Manners, Marquis of Granby.

Yet the foundation stone of a new lodge room had been laid in 1741 when on February 2nd a procession was formed to level the stone, place an inscription in lead and 'at the same time drink the King and the Craft with joyful Acclamation'. It could be that this 'new building' was a room at the Castle Inn or in an adjoining annexe, but that for some reason they did not occupy these premises in Dun Cow Lane until 1768. Whatever the reason behind this event we have at least these words to show that having a local masonic meeting place was an early desire of the brethren here.

> This Fabrick is Erected For a Lodge of Freemasons,
> In the Year of Masonry 5741 Annoque Domini 1741
> In ye 15th year of the reign of King George ye Second . . .
> Honi soit Qui Mal y Pense.

By 1781 the publican concerned, George Nicholson, moved to a house in Old Elvet and an appropriate minute records what happened.

> 3rd April. As Bro. Geo. Nicholson quits the House in which he now lives on Monday next and goes to a House in Old Elvet it is agreed that the Furniture and everything belonging to this lodge shall be removed to such House against the next general Lodge when this Lodge will agree for a proper Room to hold their meetings with Bro. Nicholson.

In 1791 and 1798 further thought was given to the issue of having a special masonic hall but it was another decade before a Bro Thomas Dunn is recorded as having 'informed the Lodge that he was empowered by Bro Thomas Richardby to offer a piece of Ground (free of every expense) for the purpose of building a lodge room and other conveniencies for the use of the Granby Lodge . . . ' This land at the riverside end of the Chapel Passage was accepted on October 9th, 1810, by two lodge members—the PGM (Sir Ralph Milbanke) and Alexander Logan (the Deputy PGM) who was also WM of the Marquis of Granby Lodge. On the 25th of

View of the temple looking west. The hammer beam roof and Gothic style doorway are prominent features.

the same month 'a Provincial Grand Lodge was opened when the Brethren walked in procession to lay the (next) Foundation Stone . . . ' It is of interest to relate that since only light refreshments—biscuits and a drink—were served at the end of regular lodge meetings the dinners to celebrate the Festivals of St John in June and December were still held at a local inn.

It was a clergyman, the Revd G. R. Bulman, who gave notice in 1865 that at the next general meeting of the lodge he would move 'that in the opinion of this lodge it is highly expedient that increased accommodation should be afforded to the members by the enlargement or alteration of the present building.' In the event it was found that the existing walls would not support a new roof and a move to a new site altogether was agreed. By 1868 the committee had the pleasure to report that 'a site had been contracted for by the RW Provincial Grand Master which the Committee strongly recommends the Lodge to purchase'. It was singular that on its acceptance the man appointed as architect was a Bro Ebdy whereas the architect for the first hall had been a Bro Ebdon. What was specially far-seeing was that a clause was inserted in the conveyance of the site 'giving any other lodge should one be properly constituted in the City of Durham the right of using the proposed new building.'

By 1 September, 1868, the property at No 36, Old Elvet had been purchased and on 22 December the 'brethren formed a procession and walked from the lodge (in

The temple looking east with a fine array of chairs.

The unusual entrance in Old Elvet.

Chapel Passage) to the site of the new Masonic Hall when the foundation stone was laid by the WMBro W. A. Malcolm with full Masonic honours'. The Durham County Advertiser gave a full description of the event remarking on the members in full Masonic costume and white kid gloves with the band of the North Durham Militia at their head. Dr Boyce's anthem, *I have built thee a house to dwell in* was sung as the stone was prepared, whilst *Rule Britannia* was played during the descent of the upper onto the lower stone with its treasures.

The ceremony concluded with the customary scattering of corn, wine and oil, an address by the acting Chaplain, a collection for the workmen and a procession once more to the previous hall. What must not be overlooked is a request made to the architect 'to proceed with the building of the Hall with all possible dispatch'. To round off the evening a banquet was held at the Three Tuns Hotel.

The building which resulted from this day is the one the visitor can see himself. In a street and part of Durham that is itself a most pleasant reminder of part of the city's history the present home of the Marquis of Granby Lodge very much holds its own. As one walks up Old Elvet from the centre of the city the façade immediately strikes one with its compact, diverse and intriguing features. The main structure is as described in the newspaper account of the stone-laying—'executed in dressed ashlar from the Brasside quarries. The style of architecture is early geometrical Gothic. The portico, forming the principal entrance, will be supported by four polished red granite columns. Above the columns on each side is a rampant lion . . . ' The shield held by the lion on the left shows an emblem and motto—Essaye—taken from the arms of the Earl of Zetland who was then the MW the Grand Master, while that on the right contains a device used by the family of John Fawcett, the Provincial Grand Master at the period of the hall's construction.

The spandrels that appear over the arched doorway and at the head of the bay window are filled with masonic devices. The one over the entrance door shows a triangle upon a 'glory' with an eye at its centre, whilst the one over the centre paired windows above is of a square and compasses with a shield upon them and a large G at its centre. At the apex of the doorway, over a pointed pair of what look like stone wands, is the Seal of Solomon, the interlaced triangles. With a pair of columned lancet windows flanking the entrance and another gabled window with its 'old trinity motif' above the bay the whole effect is of dignity and charm. It positively beckons a masonic student to enter and to enjoy the treasures within.

The building at first opened was a long narrow site exactly fitting the dimensions of the front portico. Below ground level were the kitchen and cellars; on the ground floor the vestibule and dining hall; on the first floor ante rooms and a lodge room all topped off with two attic bedrooms reached by a staircase from the room behind the bay window. Open fireplaces provided the necessary heating and the lighting was by gas. It was thus that Durham masons knew it until about 1912 when the acquisition of No 35 Old Elvet enabled the ground floor to be much enlarged and improved. It is thus that the present visitor gets an immediate impression of space and length and not least if the door to the ample dining room on the ground floor is left open.

The main impact of this vista is made by the foot of the impressive mid-Victorian staircase which is almost 15 feet wide and is approached between two most imposing stone pillars bearing the same triple globe-shaped brackets that once discharged gas but are now converted for electricity. The heavy oak banister is offset by the white-painted attempt at tracery between the staircase posts and the first main ascent branches out into two reversed stairways that lead to the lodge room above. Meanwhile, still in the vestibule we can see the personal banner of Canon Henry Baker Tristram, DD, FRS, (1822–1906) who was Provincial Prior of Northumberland, Durham and Berwick upon Tweed. The banner is mentioned as having been discovered and presented to Halwerfolc Preceptory of Knights Templar by WBro W. Walton, a PM of Marquis of Granby Lodge No 124 on 27/7/1893. A picture of Canon Tristram is to be found on the upstairs landing.

Staying on the ground floor we pass beyond the stairway to an ample Past Masters' room on the left which also serves today as a library, and at the end of the vestibule into what can only be described as a banqueting hall. It has the same ample dimensions as the lodge room above save that here the ceiling is flat with four unobtrusive brackets supporting the roof, itself decorated with moulded roundels. The room is in fact over 45 feet long, 25 feet wide and 15 feet high. At the far end the room is lit by two almost full-length, two-light pointed windows which gives the room a most ecclesiastical or baronial air whilst in the centre of the same wall there is a fine stone, pointed doorway with another pair of pointed windows above. To add to the dignity of this large room the other walls are pannelled to half their height with some very large well-executed name boards between the panelling and the ceiling. These boards show the PMs of Marquis of Granby Lodge and at one point—during the eighteenth century—have two a year for the custom then was to change the Master at each of the Festivals of St John. On the walls there is also a picture of the Marquis of Granby himself. The whole effect, especially when laid for dinner, is very fine.

In a smaller adjoining room are two items of additional interest. One is a fine chair designed for the use of the Duke of Sussex, whilst the other was for Stephen G. Kemble, a PM of Marquis of Granby Lodge in 1818/19, who was an actor of dwarfish height but the astonishing weight of 30 stones. The chair is accordingly low from the ground but of enormous width.

Retracing our steps and mounting the staircase we come to the first floor with its own present suite of rooms. On the right are the Master's room looking out over the entrance, another robing room and preparation room for candidates. To the left is a wide pointed Gothic doorway, supported by semi-detached columns with carved capitals. In the inner typanum of the arch is a carved bas-relief figure representing Moses descending from Mount Sinai with the tablets of the Law. Here the Tyler is to be found, guarding the door of the lodge room as he should. There is also here a most fascinating display, in not unduly cared for cabinets, of many items of old masonic interest. The floorcloths are of most distinctive design and the two old aprons with their turned-up or highly decorated flaps again catch the eye. One of these is a so-called 'Baptismal' apron for a Lewis (or son of a mason) whilst another is one of the early St Cuthbert's Lodge aprons and there is also a relic of the clothing for the 1824 Chapter of Concord. It is here that one begins to savour the antiquity of the local masonry that has developed into its present forms and to step with anticipation into the adjacent lodge room.

One is again struck with the same sense of spaciousness and dignity as in the hall below, for the dimensions here are the same save that here there is an open hammer-beam roof, stained and varnished. To quote again the original descrip-

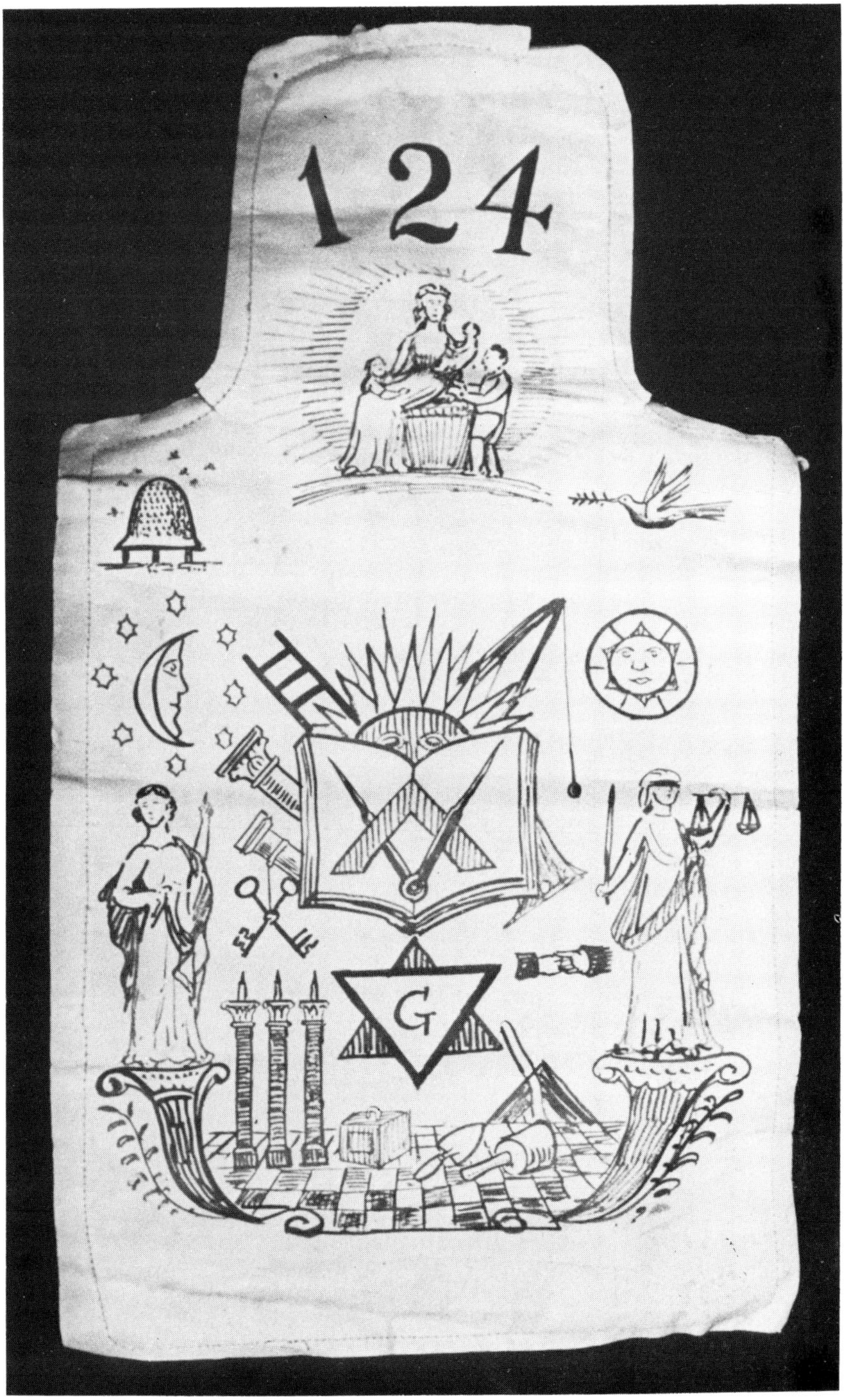

A local 'baptismal' apron for a Lewis.

tion over a century ago 'The principal beams are constructed to form an arch, supported on each side by wrought stone corbels, with masonic devices carved on the face. The room is lighted by a large five-light tracery window. A large circle with interlacing triangles forms the principal feature (of it).' We now see that the original aim of having these panes made up of leaded lights with 'Cathedral tinted glass' was not to happen but since the windows are so often covered with curtains it is not noticeable to the normal attender.

At the time of the 1936 alterations to the premises the original fireplaces which are still so noticeable elsewhere were removed 'much to the dismay of some members' but there was a very tangible link with the past in that the two oak desks for the Secretary and Treasurer, given by Bro T. W. Hearon at the time of this temple's first use, were and are retained for use. There is also something else. Amongst the array of very fine, high backed chairs that still adorn this spacious room there is a set of 3 eighteenth century chairs with decorated backs, and their appropriate office emblems (WM, SW and JW) intertwined with tracery in a trefoil at their head, which would do justice to any lordly hall. The minutes of the lodge concerning these chairs are worth recording:

On April 6th, 1773 we read:

> Likewise Bro. Wm. Stott was ordered to make a Master's Chair not to exceed £3–3–0 from the Pedestal.

By 6 January, 1775 we have: 'At the same the above brethren unanimously agreed to have a Senr. Wardens Chair and give Br Stott orders to make it', and in a minute of 5 November, 1776 it is stated:

> It is likewise agreed that Br. Stott shall make a J.W.'s Chair at his leisure but to be finished against Midsr. next.

Set as these treasures now are against the unusual pure white pedestals which they accompany and with their white fluted candlesticks before them we have here a visual passage from past to present. Their preservation and careful repair but reveals the rightful concern that Durham masons in Old Elvet have for the treasures which have been bequeathed to them.

The 'Kemble Chair'. Made for Stephen Kemble, a Past Master of Marquis of Granby Lodge, who weighed more than 30 stone.

HUDDERSFIELD

The Hall in Fitzwilliam Street

IT LOOKS AT first sight like the very substantial home of a successful Huddersfield cloth merchant and only the plain and cleary printed board across the centre of the main entrance leaves you in no doubt. It reads FREEMASONS HALL. Its blue panels, five steps to the street and the blue painted ironwork that flanks them and protects the whole front of the house may also suggest its real purpose but many a passer-by could easily imagine that this was just onc more of those fine Victorian stone and brick residences which now adorn so much of these Pennine towns. A mason of the operative kind could take pride in the delicate scroll work that tops the door pillars and supports the canopy over the entrance, and the five tall sash windows that grace the façade are also well constructed with stone surrounds and, in the upper storey, each capped with a tell-tale keystone. The whole appearance is one of stability and graciousness and now that smoke-laden air no longer darkens the brickwork something of the original colour and style more easily emerge.

The original hall behind this facade was not a very large one. It stretched only as far as the present central foyer with two rooms branching off from the central hallway, some stairs and a temple and dining room above. It was, as we shall see, handsomely conceived but what is more interesting for the moment is the circumstances which led to its being completed in the first place. A word or two about the background will make clear how things developed.

The Lodge of Truth, now No 521 on the register of the Grand Lodge of England, held its first meeting in December 1845 at the White Hart Inn, in Cloth Hall Street. The members of this lodge were not the first masons in Huddersfield for 5 of them belonged to a lodge numbered 356 and there were four others who also belonged to another local unit. These other lodges were the Lodge of Harmony which began its life in Halifax, and the Huddersfield Lodge of local vintage. These bodies, like the Lodge of Truth, met in public accommodation, and by 1855 the Lodge of Truth had moved to the George Hotel and then the Rose and Crown. Though their location might change the lodge had begun to establish its identity with its belongings. The VSL still in use by the brethren has an inscription declaring that this is the same copy as that presented at its consecration. Its donor, Bro Brook, Prov GDC, and a local stationer, also supplied the necessary cash and minute books, whilst Bro Jacques started the lodge off with 'an essential number of Aprons', and Bros Kilner, Thewlis and Turner provided the necessary jewels and the mallets. The lodge room first used was 'large but rather low', with a long table down the centre, the masonic emblems laid out on it and the brethren seated on both sides. By July 1846 the Festival of St John saw the brethren: 'sat down to a sumptuous banquet ... and the evening was spent in a joyous ebullition of masonic feeling.'

The three lodges increasingly worked together at charity allocations, a 'union' lodge of instruction, sharing special feasts and celebrations, and, if necessary, offering temporary accommodation to each other. For the Lodge of Truth this was most certainly a most important period of its life for when the lodge moved to the Rose and Crown, where the landlord, George Reid, was also the secretary, there were only 19 members. Five years later there were 89! Thirty-three initiations took place in one year, a new hall (or extension) to the hotel was erected to house the masons—and dedicated—and, as the lodge board in the present dining room upstairs makes clear it was at this point that there was initiated that 'George Frederick Samuel Robinson, commonly called VISCOUNT GODERICH, Member of Parliament, residing at No 5 Whitehall Yard, London, aged 25 years'. This was to be that Marquis of Ripon who was duly to become the MW Grand Master and then, on his conversion to Roman Catholicism, to resign from that high office. It is an association with this lodge—and the present hall in which he met so often—that is certainly memorable and unforgettable.

It was on 6 February, 1852, that the Worshipful Master, Bro Bentley Shaw, 'instigated to the act by his zealous and generous Senior Warden [another Robinson], then presented the lodge with an elegant and splendid Masonic Chair, for the WM of the time being.' Thomas Robinson, the SW, then presented another chair for the occupant of his office in future, and Past Master Johnson did likewise with the superb chair for the Junior Warden. These are the chairs that we can still see in the present large temple in Fitzwilliam Street.

To give an idea of the sheer weight of business dealt with by the Lodge of Truth at this time it is worth recording the agenda for 7 May, 1852:

> Business commenced at 2:30 p.m. with a nomination of Mr John Kirk for initiation, 'the reason being a strong desire on his part to be present at the forthcoming opening and dedication of a new Lodge Room (in July), he being at the same time both Architect and Builder'.
>
> They move up to the 2° and 3°, when four Fellowcrafts were separately raised to the sublime degree of Master Mason. Closed in these degrees to allow Test Questions from 1° to 2°.
>
> Opened in 2° for 3 separate Passings.
>
> Short break of 20 minutes for 'refreshment'.
>
> Back to labour for another Passing. Then back to the 1° for more Test Questions and up to the 2° for 3 more Passings.
>
> Closed in the 2° and then John Kirk was balloted for, elected and regularly initiated. Another initiation followed!
>
> The WM then presented to Lodge of Truth a Banner on behalf of Bro PM Schlesinger (and this is still preserved in the present Hall). A well-bound Book of Bye-laws and Book of Constitutions was also presented, and
>
> Three propositions for Initiation and Joining led to 10 p.m. when the lodge was adjourned until the following Monday!!

With a lodge that had such a flourishing membership, if a somewhat daunting agenda for its meetings, it may appear that all was going well. Yet a cloud appears on the horizon. On 7 October, 1853 the minutes record that 'the Worshipful Master with great pleasure informed the brethren that, in conjunction with PMs

Sykes and Johnson and others they had had an interview with Bro Reid, on the subject of his having let his room for an improper purpose, at the close of which Bro Reid consented that such an arrangement should be set aside.' There is also entry of a proposition 'That the best thanks of the Lodge are due and hereby presented to those Brethren who so promptly came forward to prevent the room being desecrated by Infidel Lectures'. The lecturer was a Mr Holyoak.

We do not know what exactly the nature of these 'offensive' lectures may have been but the incident caused the brethren to think seriously about moving. By August 1854 it was unanimously agreed that 'the Surplus and Benevolent Fund of the Lodge be invested in the hands of Trustees for the purpose of building a new Masonic Hall'. In October the WM, and Past Masters Robinson and Thewlis, were nominated as those names were to be inscribed on the lease for the new hall, and in November a still further step was taken. On the 3rd it was 'Proposed that the two other lodges in the Town be invited to attend and assist us in laying the foundation stone of the new Masonic Hall . . . ' and by an amendment it was also agreed that the brethren attend in masonic clothing and the Provincial Grand Master be asked to lay the stone. The date chosen was the Festival of St John, 1854, the ceremony took place and the brethren gave legal notice of their intention to quit the Rose and Crown at their meeting in January 1855.

It may well have been because of these events that the installation of Lord Goderich was deferred until June of that year, by which time the severance from Bro Reid's establishment had taken place and even items like the new organ had been removed from the precious lodge room. The Province granted a dispensation for the noble Master to be absent from the lodge when it actually removed to Fitzwilliam Street; the Master sent a cheque towards the Building Fund from Scotland; but he was back with them when the first regular lodge meeting took place in the new 'home' on 5 October, 1855.

Before we actually take a tour of the hall which is now the permanent centre of masonic activity hereabouts it is worth recording a few more facts that will explain the presence in the hall of certain items.

A committee was established to oversee the furnishing of the temple and its other adjacent rooms and in addition to the masonic floor cloth, rough ashlar and 'elegant stone tobacco box with masonic emblems' that they brought from the previous location (as well as items already referred to) we read that within a twelvemonth they had also acquired 'a beautiful square, a brass kettle, and its stand, bell and boot-jack, a dressing glass, and ink-stand, monitor or timepiece, an umbrella stand, a chart of masonic explanations and money towards the formation of a masonic library'. With this kind of 'domestication' it is hardly surprising to read that by 18 July they had selected Bro J. Lee of the Huddersfield Lodge 'as a fit and proper person . . . to reside in the new premises and to act as Tyler for that Lodge of Truth'. His appointment was duly confirmed on the usual terms, *viz* rent free, coals, gas, water and rates free. It is when we read such details that we begin to understand why, from the moment that a visitor steps inside the door, the premises have, even today, when no resident caretaker is around, a real sense of this hall being a 'home' with its panelled walls, its hallway and its carpeted reception area.

By 1857 the first application for another tenancy was received from the Knight Templars who had moved from Halifax, and they were accepted at a rent of £1 per annum! The Chamber Lobby is referred to in 1861 when a cupboard with drawers for keeping aprons was mooted, and some of the drawers still seen also came with the Lodge of Harmony when it joined the brethren here from South Parade in 1929. Indeed, we read of the local sense of fraternity when, in April 1862, the use of the Fitzwilliam Street premises was offered temporarily to Harmony whilst repairs were carried out to their own temple. In December 1862 several of the Harmony brethren attended a meeting of Truth Lodge and presented the Master and brethren with 'an elegant and beautiful silver snuff box, with an explanatory inscription engraved thereon expressing the comfort and pleasure they had experienced in using' this hall.

Not, as I have intimated above, that the first building here was exactly the one we see today. In 1868 there were further discussions to consider a further extension to what existed by using the spare land to the rear. It took until 1873 for plans and specifications to be submitted and for a rebuilding sub-committee to be authorised to spend up to £1174, that being the acceptable tender for the work. At the same time the lease which had been for 60 years was altered for one of 999 years though the annual ground rent was raised to one of £11 6s 0d! The actual opening of the vastly increased temple that now exists was on the last Friday of January, 1874.

It is into this completed hall that we now enter today. To the right of the entrance hall with its inner swing doors giving a sense of privacy and warmth we turn into what is now a useful committee room with a small glass-fronted library belonging to the Lodge of Truth. Here are kept the complete minute books, the rare copies of the lodge history and other special possessions of the lodge.

Opposite is another room of the same dimensions which has also been well-maintained and which has its own special feature. Around the upper half of the three walls that have no window is an arcade of moulded semicircles in each of which appears a masonic scene. The pictures are mainly connected with the Craft and the Royal Arch but there is a scene of Joppa which would appeal to Mark Masons and one of the Ark and the rainbow that would speak in its own way to Royal Ark Mariners. The pictures have been well renovated and were first executed by a brother who created them in thankfulness for the generous relief which was extended to him by the brethren of the Lodge of Truth. They had commissioned him to paint the large frescoes we shall meet in the main Temple. As examples of masonic symbolism the scenes here are of unique interest and it would well repay any visitor to spend a little time trying to understand the contents of the several scenes, especially if he happens to be a member of the orders mentioned. The decoration was at one stage likely to have been neglected and allowed to fade but better counsels prevailed and today these cartoons themselves mark out this hall as distinctive.

Moving back into the hallway we cannot avoid the two great pillars which stand at the outside entrance to the great temple that was added to the rear of the original building. They are some ten feet or so in height and are of Egyptian design with bright colours for their several features. The fluted stem is of gilded wood on a square wooden base, and at the top of the pillars is a silver chapiter made up of 'pods'. Leaves as of the lotus flower are reproduced in red and green, and surmounting the chapiter is a globe of some 12″ diameter covered with simulated netting. The globes are of course of terrestrial and celestial design for the respective pillars. On the square bases are two small brass plaques that give the same message: 'Presented to the Lodge of Harmony by A. W. Denton WM 1910). Designed by J. W. Cockin.' They are most attractive items and they prepare the visitor (as at Exeter, see Vol one in this series) for the delights of what he finds within.

As you pass the oak doors into the main temple you may well find yourself amazed at the dimensions. The temple reaches to the whole height of the rest of the hall which is two storeys, and is longer than it is high. A sense of height and space is enhanced by the arched, hammer-beam style of roof timbers that cover the whole of the central area and, without chairs, as it is normally seen, it looks surprisingly extensive for what was, at its first opening, a meeting place for one local lodge—though its growing membership must be recalled. Before you reach the central area, however, you must pass through an oblong area behind the Senior Warden's chair and this has a lower ceiling as it runs below the upstairs landing that was part of the original building. It is decorated at the corners, where it opens out into the larger space, with beautifully re-decorated mouldings showing many musical instruments picked out in green and white. They relieve the otherwise plain walls at this point and lead the eye naturally towards the many other wall decorations that surround the temple.

These are all of the same form of presentation, being carved and placed on the moulded heads of artificial pillars that run along the north and south walls. Running from the north-west corner to the north-east they include:

> A maul and chisel; a pentagon amongst leaves; a coil of rope, or a cable-tow; the Seal of Solomon; the Euclid diagram with the words *Aude, Vide, Tace*; and a skull and crossbones.

From the south-east to the south-west corner they are:

> A square, level and plumbline; an hour-glass; a triple tau within an irradiated upturned triangle; acacia leaves; a keystone with a triangle; and finally a heart, cross and anchor.

Above these symbols is yet another and more extensive set of painted roundels that cover all the walls of the main space and are as follows:

> North-west wall: an eye inside a triangle.
> North wall: a key, two hands clasped in greeting; 3 figures representing the virtues; the circle flanked by two parallels; and the VSL.
> East wall: an upturned square and a pair of compasses.
> South wall: a Past Master's jewel; a single pillar repeated 3 times; a single triangle; and a pair of interlaced triangles; with
> South west wall: a scene depicting Shibboleth.

Yet this array of individual items, which must surely have occupied the attention of many an interested brother during the ceremonies conducted here, is not the only decoration.

At the east end of the hall is a raised dais on which stands the Master's chair behind a large pedestal. The chair is inscribed as having been presented to the Lodge of Truth by the Master (1856), Cross Marsh, in 1875 and it certainly occupies well the elevated place it possesses. Above the chair however is a huge semicircular painting on the east wall, surmounting the curtains that hang below it. The picture is surrounded by seven huge stars and depicts the sleeping figure of Jacob from whose side there rises a large ladder towards heaven, itself flooded with celestial light and showing angels ascending and descending thereon. It is unlike the usual tracing board in that there are no pillars and pedestals or VSL displayed.

At the west end of the hall, and on the surface that mounts above the pillars bearing the musical instruments is another huge circular scene which is only visible to those who stand in front of the Senior Warden's chair. Here we see an imposing Old Father seated on a throne with the scythe, an hourglass beside him and the All-Seeing eye above. In the band of the picture's frame are the signs of the Zodiac

Looking east with the special chequered carpet and 'Jacob' picture over the Master's chair.

and suffusing the whole picture is the light of the sinking sun—a fitting indication for its place in the west. At the foot of the picture are, on the left as you look at it, three birds, whilst on the right is an owl.

The other feature of this room is that facing the Junior Warden's pedestal but firmly set into the north wall is a wooden armchair which is used by the Director of Ceremonies. This, so far as I am aware, is only repeated in one place that I have shown in these volumes (see Bath, Vol one).

The coloured ceiling of the apparently vast room is also coloured like the pillars outside and carries three huge roundels between the roof timbers. There are two panels with interlaced triangles and one with the pentagram. The whole effect as you stand back and consider it is very remarkable. It is so unexpected after the homely nature of the rest of the property or from the outside appearance, and one can appreciate that filled with brethren and some of the other features of the lodges that meet here—especially the oldest and largest tracing boards—the ashlars and the tripod, not to mention the warrants and banners, this must appear even more a hall to remember.

Behind the curtains of the east wall it would be possible to see that the Victorian builders had even grander designs. The wall is a partition and could be flung back on special occasions to increase the area yet one third more. This area, which is normally reached by a corridor on the north side, was once called the 'Billiards Room' but is now more soberly referred to as the Annexe. It is large and gaunt but round its walls are some interesting objects—the banner of the Hope Preceptory of the Knights Templars bearing the 'Halig Fax' (or Holy Face) which readers will find mentioned on the stair windows of the hall in that town; the Lodge of Truth Mark banner with its distinctive Keystone design; a banner of the Concord Lodge of 1922; and the rich colours of the Connaught banner of 1919.

Speaking of banners should remind us that the Lodge of Truth has its own fine specimen. It is shield-like on the summons but actually rectangular, with a deep blue background. At its centre, between white Yorkshire roses, is the perfect ashlar supporting the three great lights, with an all-seeing eye above and that surmounted by the Paschal Lamb that signifies a Templar connection. At the top left and right are the beehive and a sailing ship, whilst beneath the scroll bearing the words 'Veritas, Honor, Virtus' (Truth, Honour, Virtue) are the recurring symbols of an hour glass, tripod with suspended ashlar, the moon and stars, the skull and

The 'Halig Fax' banner of the Lodge of Truth.

crossbones, and the pentagram on an irradiated glory. As a piece of decoration it is well appreciated and the words of Bro Schlesinger in his letter of presentation to the WM are happily recalled:

> It shall be our constant Monitor in all our future duties. In it we shall find a perpetual admonition to practise, with still greater activity those Philanthropic and Benevolent Principles of Masonry which you so well and truly carried out when the Lodge was honoured with your Presidency.

There remains only the room upstairs which was first the lodge room and then, when the extension was built, became known as the Supper Room. It is a room that covers most of the second storey apart from a landing and preparation room at one end and it certainly is a room of distinction. The lodge boards that adorn its walls are themselves works of art with beautifully designed headpieces covering not only the lodges for the Craft but also Truth Chapter, Truth Mark Lodge and two boards of KT Preceptors. The centre piece of the ceiling is a large circular motif in gold and blue with seven stars, each placed in a circle between the parallel lines of the circle frame itself containing a gold labyrinthine pattern. Within this circle is yet another shallow domed area in which is a circle holding the Seal of Solomon in gold at the crown of the roof. Here, as they gather for dinner, brethren can indeed be reminded of both the happy present and the earlier days of this hall. It is a room with more than a century of memories.

As one leaves this hall there are just two slight but interesting items that ought to be carried away with a visitor. The first is the permanent lectern that stands in the south-east corner of the main temple and is for the use of the Chaplain—an officer in this Province who has other duties in the degrees than is often the case elsewhere. The other is a copy of a menu that is held in one of the Lodge of Truth Guard Books. It was produced for a Special Social of Celebration on 23 November, 1918 and it reads as follows:

MENU
Peace Soup
Submarines interned
British Bulwarks — Turkish Delight and Zeppelins
Spuds a la Empire
Americaine Tartelette — Colonial Cheese
Allied Salad — Italian Cream
Armistice à la Français

KINGSTON UPON HULL

The Hall in Daggard Lane

If in this volume the masonic hall that can claim to be the oldest purpose-built structure in continuous occupation is the one at Sunderland then the second is undoubtedly the one in Kingston upon Hull. The hall there has been in constant use since 1804. The Minerva Lodge, now No 250, which has been resident there throughout was the only one of the five original lodges to survive. The lodge first met at the appropriately named 'Masons Arms' in Chapel Lane following its inauguration in 1783 and by 1784 had arranged for its chairs in the east, west and south to be made after the pattern of those in the Grand Lodge at York. In 1798 the fine silver Jewel still worn by the Treasurer had been purchased and Thomas Fletcher presented a 'painting of the Floor Cloth'. In 1800 the members of Minerva must have been amongst the 300 brethren who attended the dedication of the Freemasons Hall in Mytongate built by the masons of Rodney Lodge and

The east of the temple. Of interest is the inscribed arch, the large globes and the magnificent painted ceiling.

perhaps were stirred into wanting their own premises.

In 1802 we read that the lodge was building its own temple on a piece of land belonging to the Old Chapel and adjoining edifice. The chapel itself was built in 1698 by the first nonconformist body in Hull, a Presbyterian congregation constituted in 1643, the year of the plague, the town siege and the Civil War. The site of the temple was in what first had been Hutchinson Lane and then, at about the time it was paved in 1754, became Daggard Lane or—as it is more commonly called today—Dagger Lane.

The west of the temple is dominated by the impressive organ.

The terms of occupancy were a lease of 96 years, an annual rent of £16 and the rent to be paid to the Trustees of the chapel. Originally only the first floor was to be used for masonic purposes as we read that John Medd, currier, rented the ground floor of the lodge on a lease of 30 years with a half-yearly rent. Indeed we know that whilst obligations might be taken upstairs there was a slaughter-house below, although this later became merely a warehouse. What is fascinating to note is that the lodge was to meet once a month from Lady Day to Michaelmas and twice a month for the rest of the year, the Royal Arch every first Friday, and the Knights Templar on the 1st SUNDAY after the quarter day meetings of the Royal Arch. Indeed, in 1802 there were already meeting here the three degrees of the Craft, Mark Masonry, Royal Arch, Knight Templar, Old English Harodim or Orange Masonry, and Ark, Mark and Link. The building was consecrated on 6 December, 1802.

By 11 April, 1810 the Vicar, Mr Bromby, 'presents his most respectful compliments to the Master, Wardens and Brethren of the Minerva Lodge of Freemasons, and requests from them permission on behalf of himself and a few other patronizers and performers of Sacred Music to meet occasionally for practice in their room'. Permission was given and in July the traffic was returned—for there was a procession to the church in honour of the birthday of the Prince Regent. There was no conflict between Church and Craft then it seems!

The bust of Frank Appleyard behind the Junior Warden's chair.

In 1819, October, a Bro Crompton proudly presented to the lodge an oil painting of the Good Samaritan which was to hang over the Poor Box. It had been painted by his daughter who clearly understood and encouraged one of the lasting characteristics of a freemason's heart. It showed that the adornment of the lodge room was a constant care of the brethren and on 23 May, 1821 Bro Crow presented a silk flag in memory of the late Bro Viscount Horatio Nelson (cf. the Stone at Gt Yarmouth, Vol 2). Silver and glassware such as can be seen in the display case between the two present lodge room entrances now began to be presented but what especially endears the main temple here to the author is the record that on 22 June, 1825, Bro George Oliver, DD delivered the First Lecture within these walls.

The prominent pillars outside the main temple with Hebrew names. Above the entrance is a cypher greeting.

Above: *A view of the painted ceiling with signs of the Zodiac and in each corner there are emblems of the degrees.* Below: *The All-Seeing-Eye and rays above the Master's chair.*

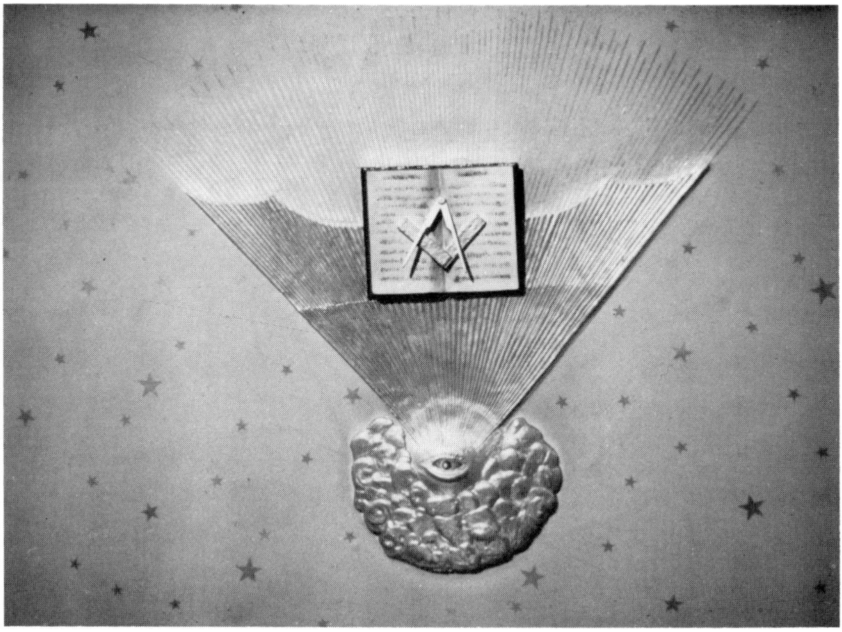

Masons ever being mindful of their responsibility towards others who were not masons it is encouraging to read that it was in 1830 that a subscription was raised towards the stained glass windows in Holy Trinity Church nearby, whereas it was 1843 before the lodge room received its first major repair, painting and decorating. Now began to appear those busts which are so striking a feature of this Temple, first the ones of Ajax and Homer, and then one of Lord Zetland, MWGM, fashioned by Bro Thomas Earle, whose son in law, Frank Appleyard, seems to have been the man responsible for the design of the original temple. Thomas Earle's own bust is situated to the left of the Senior Warden's chair whilst one of Appleyard himself is behind the Junior Warden.

It was time by 1863 for another entire renovation of the premises and so extensive were the improvements that it was felt that a re-consecration with full ceremonies was required. It was perhaps now that some of the present features began to make their permanent appearance for the mosaic carpet was presented by Humber lodge, Bro G. Hardy gave the three large tracing boards that now adorn the temple walls, a valuable flagon and two cups were presented to the KT Conclave and a complete set of Officers' collars and gauntlets, as well as a bookcase and books to go in it, were received. Even the handsome Square and compasses that lie on the VSL were a gift from Bro J. Brooke, SW, in November 1873.

The hall was now about to take another large step forward for in January 1874 not only was the lodge able to purchase the freehold from the chapel trustees but the chapel itself was up for sale and was added to the existing hall to make the present premises. At last the masons could claim to be masters in their own house and they were also able to add a dining room, kitchen and ancillary offices to the somewhat limited facilities hitherto. The old dining room, with its particular character has now become a second lodge room though it is mostly enjoyed for the Knight Templar and other degree ceremonies, for which it is admirably suited. Its fireplace, flat and lower ceiling, its old prints and unusual statuary, not to mention its period furniture, all lend a distinctive atmosphere to the room. It must have been a very pleasant place in which to dine: it is most certainly a very fitting place in which to hold a unique black-hatted Preceptory.

The Junior Warden's chair.

The impressive organ.

The life of the hall was not as secure however as the late Victorian occupiers must have imagined it. Despite the constant maintenance and serious repair after the ravages of World War II the local authorities threatened this ancient hall and its environs with demolition after compulsory purchase. Hardly, but happily, the whole scheme was fought and at last the most desired outcome was granted. In December 1986—so recently—the hall was declared a protected building of major historical value and its future does at last seem wholly secured short of a major natural disaster. The brethren could thus turn to the task of really establishing their possessions and the result of their labours is now a delight for all visitors to savour. We have here a modern presentation of an ancient and much respected temple.

Entering today by the simple doorway in Dagger Lane, which itself retains so much of an older Kingston upon Hull, you find yourself at once in an atmosphere of well-ordered Freemasonry. The stairs to the right rise above essential offices and to the left you are soon aware of the large bar and dining room that was once the warehouse of an earlier age. At the top of the winding stairs you come to a modest landing area and immediately in front of you stand two most intriguing objects. They are the two pillars of B and J, bearing their proper names in Hebrew within a gilded, irradiated frame on the black background, and they stand on two well shaped ashlars of bluish marble. At the head of each of the pillars is a flat plinth and above this a plain golden ball. The pillars stand at the approach to a white door in a curved recess and on the flat face of the recess roof and between the globes are three words in masonic coded writing which read, 'Brother, welcome here'. The surrounding décor of pale grey walls, pure white skirting and door panels, together with the striking chequered carpeting, makes a most impressive impact on the visitor. Here is age joined with modern furnishing.

The temple that awaits you on the other side of the door is all of a piece. The overall effect is of a sizeable but yet restrained room of blue and white. Facing you in the east is a huge semicircular arch that appears at first sight to run from floor to ceiling and down again. On further notice the arch is supported on two other black and gold pillars which fit snugly into the north and south walls. The actual stonework of the arch is white but it is so slender that it hardly disrupts the continuity of the blue ceiling of the main part of the room with the blue half dome of the apse which extends further to the east. It is this happy design which gives a real sense of the blue infinity of the firmament and this is of course enhanced by the massive circle on the main ceiling, depicting the zodiac figures with their stars in their constellations all round. The ceiling is a most impressive sight, and yet soothing to one who sits beneath it for a ceremony.

On closer examination we can see certain other features. Around the arch are the letters I T N O T G A O T U and between the T and G there is a keystone which bears a letter I (is this perhaps an attempt at the Hebrew letter YOD which stands for the Almighty? or is it the first letter of another name for the keystone?). Above the keystone and on a patterned blue border that separates the cornice from the ceiling proper there is a delicate painting of an eye with light radiating from it. Seemingly, below the keystone, but in fact on the apex of the apse roof behind it, there is still more striking design—another eye at the centre of a large gilded boss and from the eye a great fan of rays shining upon the VSL with the square and compasses extended on the open pages.

At the east end of the temple and below this expanse of blue sky and roof we cannot avoid the imposing arrangement of 20 ft high pillars that reach from floor to cornice and frame first the old light brown chairs for WM, IPM and Chaplain (the latter being on the right of the Master) with the Minerva Lodge banner above them. The blue draped curtains that hang behind the chairs and banner add to the effect already created by the ceilings. Around the base of the apse roof and above these pillars, as also round the whole room there runs a brown frieze with gold lettering. The inscription in Latin is as follows:

North wall from West to East

AVDI. VIDE. TACE—FIAT LVX ET LVX FVIT-QUAERITE ET INVENIETIS
(hear, see, be silent—let there be light and there was light—seek and ye shall find).

East wall from West to South

LVMEN INGENS ORIENTE LVCET VBI PAX ET SILENTIVM REGNANT
(a great light shines in the east where peace and silence reign)

South wall from East to West

LVX LVCET TENEBRIS SED TENEBRAE NON EAM COMPREHENDERVNT
(the light shineth in the darkness and the darkness comprehended it not)

The chairs are original and are superb examples of the best early Victorian design with upholstered seats and backs, side pillars of the Corinthian, Ionic and Doric designs, and the motifs of the various officers carved in roundels at their head. The arms of the chairs finish with busts of female figures in the Master's chair and the heads of beasts for the other two. The Wardens' chairs in their normal places have the same carved arms as the Master's, their own motifs of level and plumbline on black-based roundels, but with large rich red cushions to ease the less ample occupants of these otherwise large chairs. As we have seen elsewhere the steps to these chairs are graded, one step for the Junior Warden, two for the Senior and three for the Master.

The partly ecclesiastical look of the room is created by what at first might look like two great panels of the Ten Commandments that hang the whole length of the wall between the pillars to the left and right of the Master's dais. They are of course the original boards, beautifully inscribed, naming the Masters of Minerva lodge from its inception. They are already complete. Furthermore the seats for PMs and senior visitors below them and along the east wall are formed like canons' stalls in a cathedral with curved backs and projecting arms, all fixed to the wall. As a photograph shows the effect is very fine.

In the west the effect is almost repeated save that there is only the SW's chair and pedestal against the backdrop of pillars, full length boards (the centre one here denoting the names of the Chapter Principals) and grey walls with blue ceiling above. To the right of the SW, as he sits, there is the very imposing and well-tuned pipe organ with its fine pipe case and hooded console beneath. The organ casing reaches almost to the ceiling and adds noticeably to the quality and sense of well-being in this room.

We cannot leave this fascinating meeting place without looking at the walls and ceiling once more. Mention has already been made of the terracotta busts that grace the gentle niches (in blue of course!) and these are interspersed with four of the lodge's oldest possessions—the large tracing boards of the three Craft degrees and of the Royal Arch. Though obviously fine examples of Harris (with their miniature copies beneath them) they are also noteworthy for being on open display all the time and thus a matter for constant speculation by the brother sitting in lodge. Though not frequently seen the Chapter board is on similar display in both Newport and Faversham (see the volume on Halls in the South).

Above these boards and the cornice that separates walls from ceiling there runs a frieze of patterned blue on which are painted a number of large shields indicating the main aspects of Freemasonry practised in Hull from earliest times. Here we find a head of Minerva, the separate arms of the premier and Antients Grand Lodges, that of the Mark Grand Lodge, two of the A and A Rite, and one for the KT. To understand these arms and be able to identify and explain them is yet a further inducement to local masons to be making "a daily advancement". Whilst from within the zodiac already mentioned on the roof itself there suspends, from a red central moulding bearing a gold pentacle, a slender chain carrying a chandelier with four lights. By its illumination you now perceive that at the four corners of the blue firmament are the glorious sun, the moon and stars, a skull and crossbones and the united pick, shovel and crowbar. The whole ceiling area, like the walls and the totally chequered floor, bear countless objects and images that speak out the full-bodied messages of an ancient fraternity.

As we leave this old lodge room we could spend even more time looking at the rest of the treasures in this now well-restored building . . . the trio of Master, JW's and Treasurer's chairs in the old dining room, the almost unique charter for the Encampment of the KT which meets here, the two very old Warden's pillars that now stand on the table in the upper changing room, and the portraits, old jewels and Kirkwall scroll that grace the landing.

We cannot leave, however, without remarking on the Chapter treasures. On the 5 April, 1860 the minutes record that Companion Sparrow of the Chapter who was the Collector of Customs at Hull made a presentation of the set of heraldic Banners of the Twelve Tribes of Israel. These are in the form of small metal discs or shields and are unusual not only for their general appearance but also because the emblems they bear are surrounded by a latin inscription, the details of which are as follows:

1. ACCUMBIT UT LEO—lion couchant, sword, sceptre
2. ACCUMBENS INTER TERMINOS—an ass
3. IN LITTORE MARIS HABITAT—a ship
4. AQUARUM INSTAR RUENS—waves
5. VASA INIQUITATIS BELLANTIA—sword & halberd in saltire
6. IPSE TANDEM PREVINCET—lion on a flag
7. AMANS TRITURAE—a bullock
8. RAMUS FECUNDUS JUXTA FONTEM—a vine
9. MANE COMEDET PRAEDAE VESPERE DIVIDET SPOLIA—a wolf

10. COLUMBIA IN VIA—a horse with a snake at its heels
11. PRAEBEBIT DELICIAS REGIBUS—a flagon and cup
12. CE(R)VA EMISSA—a hind

These are still in use at the chapter ceremonies.

Here is indeed another hall to remember and one in which its occupants can take the fullest pride. It is a matter for profound satisfaction that both the fabric and the contents can be retained as part of this country's past and future. For those who have the privilege of attendance at the ceremonies worked here it is no less a memorable experience than the viewing of its contents. Long may we have such halls as that in Dagger Lane!

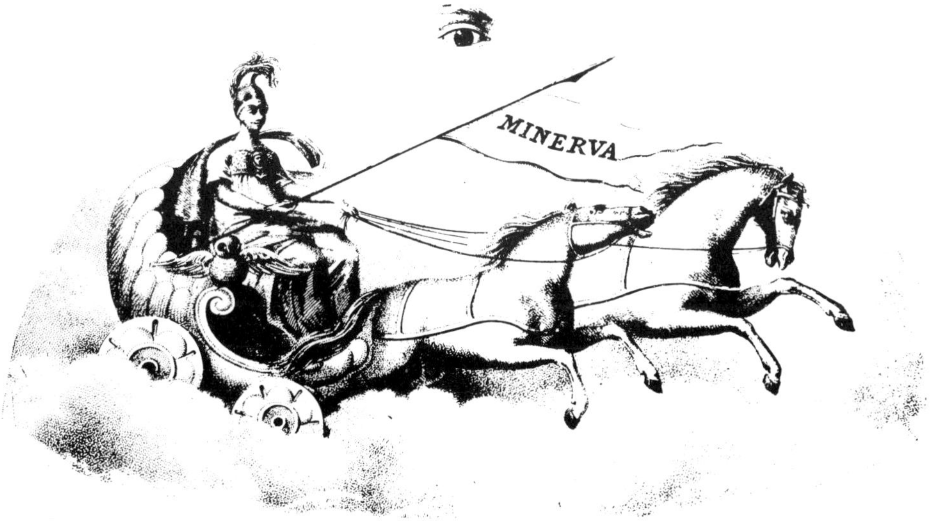

One of the wall decorations of the lesser temple.

LIVERPOOL

The New Masonic Hall in Hope Street's Old Garden

THE MASONIC STRANGER in Liverpool could hardly be surprised at what he finds in the principal hall of the Craft in that city. The façade is worthy of a building that houses the headquarters of the largest Craft Province in England and Wales and the interior undoubtedly lives up to the promise suggested by the outside appearance. It is especially worth noting that to gain admission to this hall the visitor passes through a fine oak doorway set between two Doric pillars which support, above their pediment, a shell-like recess with the enfoliated coat of arms of the United Grand Lodge of England and the words acquired from the Antients Grand Lodge—*Kodesh Lo Adonai*—meaning 'Holiness to the Lord'. That seems a very fitting motto for a building that is set in the street uniting two of England's newest Cathedrals, and which has for long been a meeting place for those who might otherwise have ever found themselves set at a perpetual distance. The fact that the doorway is completed with a crenellated arch bearing a fine keystone has its own extra message for many masons and is also not without special meaning in the world of today.

The present building is the result of continual progress during the last 130 years towards improving the facilities for as many lodges as possible in the area to find a masonic home whilst also providing for those special occasions which must be associated with a large Province. The story of that growth is in itself a memorable one and deserves a brief mention.

As with all masonic life in the growing centres of English eighteenth and nineteenth century development the earlier custom of using inns and taverns was no longer practicable for the membership of lodges in this increasingly busy and prosperous trading port. Lancashire showed the great increase in lodges and their membership by being divided into the provinces of East and West in 1825. Already, as early as 1809, the brethren of lodge No 20, the mother lodge of the still extant Harmonic Lodge No 216, did attend a Freemasons Hall at the top of Bold Street, Liverpool after a function for the laying of a foundation stone of the pedestal of a statue of George III. Yet this was merely a place for refreshment after labour.

It was not until 1848 that a committee of Sincerity Lodge, No 292, was appointed to confer with other local lodges about the need to secure 'a desirable house as a Masonic Temple'. Nothing of consequence occured until 1856 when a broader group of leading brethren in the town decided on April 11th 'to take into consideration the desirability of raising a fund to build a Hall for masonic purposes'. By 21 May a trust deed had been drawn up and sites were seriously considered. Five were eventually submitted for consideration and the one that was selected was that of '22 Hope Street, consisting of a good house and large garden adjoining the Catholic Institution'. The choice of a property—the only one—with a garden space was to prove to be foresight of a high order.

Hope Street was then on the virtual periphery of the growing city and contemporary maps show but few other buildings around. At the south end of the street was an overgrown quarry, which became St James Cemetery, and there was also a mineral spring with eye-healing qualities which had led the area to be described in 1773 as 'the Spaw (Spa) at Mount Zion near Liverpool'. The mention of 'Mount Zion' locally also seems fortuitous.

Things now moved apace and though the hall committee only met for the first time on 23 April the work to adapt the house was done on time and by 8 October the hall was declared open. The Mariners, Merchants, Sincerity and Perseverance Lodges all held meetings there before the month was out. Their needs for a place were obvious and were met, but with a population rising in one century (1750–1850) from 20,000 to almost 400,000 it should be no surprise to learn that from 8 lodges in Liverpool in 1858 there were 17 in 1868 and four more by 1872. A new hall extension was already becoming a necessity, as were other services. In 1862 the committee approved the purchase of 24 spittoons, a supply of newspapers for the next three years whilst a new organ was also purchased. £30 was also spent on structural alterations.

It was now that the idea began to be mooted of using all the land belonging to the 'house in the garden' and in November 1872 Lord Skelmersdale, Deputy Provincial Grand Master, laid the foundation stone for a new scheme that was to provide a large Lodge Room, Chapter Room, Banquet Hall, Library, Committee and cloakrooms, with kitchens and cellars in the basement. It is, as you realise, this garden area being used that helps you understand today the impressive depth to the building which can hardly be imagined, even with the fine frontage. More accommodation, however, also meant more use and more attraction for masons. In 1889 no fewer than 13 lodges were formed, and by 1909 there were 29 lodges meeting on these premises, 8 in other halls and 19 more in licensed buildings. The time had come to consider seriously the re-building on a larger scale of the western, or older part of the hall, as well as modernising the accommodation around the present front of the building.

Raising the £10,000 required was not easy and some brethren thought it likely to suggest a wrong use of resources. It was a letter in the Liverpool Post and Mercury of 2 July, 1910 that sought to set all anxieties at rest. It included these words: 'The Hope Street Temple and land are their own in fee simple, easy of access, and quiet and as such, should, and please God, shall be, the headquarters of Masonry in Liverpool'. Sadly, the intervening war years brought their own natural delay and recovery after the war was slow, but by 1926 it became possible to obtain a strip of land to the side of the original façade. Looking at the present front with fresh eyes one can still see how the present entrance is set on that extra land and the blank archway to its left reveals where the earlier impressive entrance and steps led down to the street. The work was unveiled in 1932.

Thus was created the hall much as we know it today, more than 50 years later. Gone is 'the vision of a house in a garden set back from the street, partly hidden by

Top: *The Adams Room, Liverpool, with classical motifs.* Left: *Gothic style Senior Warden's chair.* Above: *The War Memorial at the entrance hall.*

stabling and a vinery, a long twisting and winding path set with flower beds and a space open to the heavens'. Now every square foot of the area is filled with brickwork and masonry so that the lodges that have met, and still meet, here can fulfil the honourable practices that shape Freemasonry.

It is into this impressive collection of suites and assembly halls that we now pass. There is much to see. The entrance hall immediately gives the sense of dignity and strength that pervades the whole structure and shows the visitor something of the dimension of the whole with its processional corridor closing in the distance with a most impressive War Memorial plaque at the head of seven stairs. The panel is flanked by two wreathed armorial bearings—one having the arms of the United Grand Lodge of England, and the other the Liver Bird with wings erect and bearing an olive branch.

Between them are the names of the fallen in the First World War, with five military figures, two at the end and three in the centre, all, unusually, looking away from the viewer. The two end figures hold, the one a sword, like a cross, on high, and the other a large wooden cross at chest level. Above the three centre men, who walk away into a recess, are the words on the Antients Grand Lodge bearings—'God is our Guide', and underneath the whole panel we read: 'These Brethren from the Lodges in Liverpool and District, Inspired by High Ideals, when the call of duty came, laid down their lives in the Great War, passed into the Great Silence, for they loved the Brotherhood.'

With such a reminder from the First Degree Charge we can rightly make our way through the corridors and stairways that lead us from one distinctive room into another. The Ionic room is naturally the most stark and when its central partition is pushed back it also serves as a sizeable ballroom. As may be expected of these newer rooms the furniture has been specially designed to suit the whole décor and the WM's chair here is of the style of Ionic entablature.

We pass into the Doric suite with its more imposing three-stepped dais in the east, its massive set of three chairs for the WM, IPM and the Senior officer present, and separate Wardens' chairs—that of the SW given in memory of the first initiate, Canon Coup, in 1924, and that of the Junior Warden coming from Alliance Lodge No 667, founded in 1856. This lodge room also has tracing boards in their box at the centre of the lodge room, and some very elegant white pillars on the Wardens' pedestal.

The Roman Room, as its name implies, suggests a spacious marbled 'aula' of some classical period. The east end has an exquisite apselike recess with a sun in glory above the central panel behind the tall Master's chair. The whole is enclosed by two large fluted columns carrying a wide sweeping arch with its keystone, and this motif is reproduced five times down each wall with medallions in the spandrels and a deep cavity ceiling. The chairs flanking that of the WM are two country-made chairs of eighteenth century design with splayed rear legs. As is common in this part of the country the rough and smooth ashlars are still kept at the NE and SE corners of the lodge carpet and here the tripod is placed at the western end of the floor with the kneeling pad on entry at its foot. The tracing board was presented by the Merchants' Lodge No 241 on the occasion of its 150th anniversary in 1930.

From Rome to Egypt is a natural step and those familiar with the Egyptian Rooms in the Great Eastern Hotel in Liverpool Street, London, will find a most

The Roman room looking east.

The Egyptian room.

worthy companion here in a temple that is most often used for RA ceremonies. The coffered ceiling, the richly-painted and foliage-bedecked pillars, the panels of Egyptian designs and especially the wide winged birds that adorn each alcove serve to give this room its warm, intimate and very separate character. The motif in the centre of each ceiling section is a pentagram and for those interested in RA arrangement it is worth noting that here the pedestal and six lights are placed at the east end of the carpet and not between the ensigns as elsewhere. The SW's chair shows in its faint lettering that it belonged to the Mariner's Lodge No 249 (founded 1783) and has a special feature. Being of Windsor type with a railed back it has an open spindle pattern in its top rail which shows seven small 'patera' (or shallow cups) representing seven stairs.

We pass next into the Adams Room which reproduces the style associated with the Adams brothers of the eighteenth century. This is a most elegant and charming room with its curved ceiling covered with varied forms of delicate white moulding. Picked out against a pale green background the effect is of being in some gracious mansion and the fan-shaped sun's rays which spring from behind the Master's chair, together with the severe but slender pairs of columns, must surely impress any candidate introduced into masonry here. The principal chairs in the east are of pseudo-Gothic design as was customary in mid-Victorian times. The triangular top rail of each is carved in low relief with ivy leaves and berries. Also striking is the tripod carrying the smooth ashlar for it must be five feet or so in height. Forming again a triangle with the other ashlars at the east end it begins to speak more eloquently of its symbolic purpose than is usually the case.

It is now time to pass into the oldest and largest lodge room of the whole complex. It is today less bedecked with wall pictures than it once was but it is none the less impressive for being now rather more sparing of those items. It is a lofty room of classical proportions, with a huge central chandelier, a balcony along the northern wall, a huge but charming clock designed in the style of the whole Grand Lodge Arms with their angelic supporters. It is particularly interesting as having the interlacing of a cable tow in the arrangement. On the balcony above the clock is a fine pipe organ.

The small railed kneeling cushions in the east are original and beside them there used to be two tripod-supported globes but these have been removed for safety to the museum. The tripod is again of more than usual size and marks its importance in lodge ceremonies, as also do the very well-preserved John Harris tracing boards that lie before it. The third degree board is special in that it carries its reference to the Royal Arch.

The three main chairs in the east are some of the hall's finest treasures. That of the WM is of oak and was presented to the Worshipful the Mayor of Liverpool, Bro Edward Samuelson, by Bro John Pearson of Sefton Lodge, No 680, to commemorate the installation of Lord Skelmersdale as PGM in the Town Hall, Liverpool, on 27 February, 1876. The two flanking chairs bear the number 294, which was that of Merchants Lodge in 1832, and all the inscriptions and symbols are clearly pre-Union for they represent also things used in other degrees than the Craft. Thus, in addition to the All-Seeing Eye, the Square and Compasses, the chequered pavement, the Five-pointed star, the Double Triangle, the Masonic Arms and the level, we find—a Pelican, a Cross, a Lamb, a Ladder with five rounds, a Serpent, a Crown, a Sword, a Fish and the number 144,000. The rails of the chair bear in Mark cypher the following inscription: 'In hoc signo vinces' and 'Innocence'. A truly remarkable example, in another medium than the usual aprons, of how other degrees were worked under the auspicies of a Craft lodge. They are chairs that bear very careful scrutiny.

The Senior and Junior Wardens' chairs are in their own way also distinctive as not being at all traditional and having been specially made by a founder of the Alliance Lodge 667, Bro W. P. Witter, and made when the lodge met first at Roby in 1856.

The items of interest possessed by lodges using this hall are not all on constant display like those already mentioned and it would be impossible to catalogue them all. It is, I believe, worth mentioning a few. Mariners Lodge have an Old Testament volume printed in 1640 and a New Testament of 1649, the antique clock which stands at the head of the main staircase, a brass square of 1819 and a punch bowl and jug decorated with masonic emblems and dedicated to a Squire Hargreaves in 1813. Their lodge jewels date from 1819 and the IPM's jewel has an unusual design but is of unknown origin. It is of such evident antiquity that Grand Lodge permits it to be worn still.

The Antient Union Lodge No 203 records that in 1799 the Senior Warden made a 'present of a Cocket Hat to be worn by the Worshipful Master in Lodge', whilst the Derby Lodge No 724 has mourning furnishings that draped the pedestals in black, provided large black rosettes for all wands and black ribbons for all columns. They were still being used in 1909.

The provisions for refreshment and the after-proceedings are as ample as would be expected in so sumptuously appointed a Masonic Hall. The main banqueting hall can seat over 200 persons in its ample and tastefully decorated surroundings, and for the masonic visitor or Liverpool mason off duty there is a similarly large and well-furnished Masonic Club room, with its own bar and eating facilities. The Club has two very interesting possessions.

The first is a silver-tipped ramshorn snuffbox which bears on the lid the engraved Coats of Arms of Grand Lodge and the Earl of Zetland, who was Grand Master when this club was founded in 1863—a fact also inscribed on this item. The other piece is a collecting box made from oak salvaged from a Spanish warship sunk at the Siege of Gibraltar in 1782. Carving on the sides show the aged and orphans in receipt of masonic relief. The ends are inlaid with the design of an anchor at one end and the square and compasses at the other.

Here then is another memorable hall in one of our country's great cities. Today it is almost at the heart of the present busy city whereas once it was on the edge. It is both modern in its present facilities and yet preserves in its walls so many relics of a freemasonry long established. It is a fine hub for the many wheels that keep this great Province turning. Those who use it have a treasure to preserve.

MANCHESTER

A Truly Memorable Freemasons' Hall

THE PEDIGREE OF Freemasonry in the area called the Province of East Lancashire is both long and honourable. It was here, in the year 1727, that a lodge is recorded as meeting at the King's Head Inn, Chapel Street, Salford and its existence was formally acknowledged at the Quarterly Communication of Grand Lodge on December 27 of that year. It was the first lodge outside London and Westminster to be entered on the Register in the capital and its foundation was soon copied by others so that in 1734 the first Province of Lancashire was established. The area of the county remained as one Province until the year 1826 when it was divided into its present Eastern and Western Divisions, with headquarters at Manchester and Liverpool respectively.

For many years thereafter all the lodges in East Lancashire met in public houses until, in 1858, several Manchester lodges, being eager to get away from licensed premises, leased some rooms in Cross Street, in the heart of the growing city. Although these 'Masonic Rooms' were used for only a limited period the move that had been made established a principle which has been upheld until the present day. All East Lancashire lodges are held away from public houses and, with a very few exceptions, meet on specially appointed masonic premises.

Thus, with the precedent set, efforts began to have a separate Manchester Freemasons' Hall and in 1864 the first one was opened by the Provincial Grand Master, RWBro Stephen Blair. The elegant façade of that hall, adorned with masonic emblems, still stands and marks a meeting place of masons which continued until 1929.

The number of Manchester lodges now began to grow apace and it was soon apparent that the facilities provided in Cooper Street were going to be increasingly inadequate. By 1909 the first public pronouncement was made in Provincial Grand Lodge that a move from the existing hall was both essential and desirable. Out of 137 lodges in the Province 48 now sought to meet in Manchester and Salford and Cooper Street could not possibly accommodate them. (It is especially relevant here to note that lodges in this part of England quite frequently meet 8 to 12 times a year and the demands on masonic premises are thus much greater than might be the case elsewhere.)

It was urged that what was required was 'a central site, somewhere within the triangle of the three great railway stations and not too far from the Royal Exchange; at least three lodge rooms would be required; suitable club premises; and the Provincial Office might be within the building.' It is worth remarking that the mention of the proximity of the railway stations shows that the motor car was

Part of the library which is sometimes used for meetings.

not yet a significant rival to the train and any thought as to its eventual parking in a fast growing city centre was not something that need even be contemplated.

What was wise was the suggestion about the Provincial Office for it was still the case that the Provincial Secretary had to rent separate rooms at 2 Cooper Street, and paid £40 per annum for the privilege. With what was an evidently busy future ahead this step of incorporating the provincial administration was to prove immensely sensible. By 1987 there were 394 lodges to be served and 159 of these meet in Manchester and Salford. It is clear that these early twentieth century masons thought hard and well about how things were likely to go.

Lord Derby, the Provincial Grand Master, expressed the view at this same Provincial meeting that whilst the time was right for such a change it was the lodges in the district that had to meet and decide whether the project was feasible. He set up a Council consisting of 12 members from all parts of the Province and he asked that they should thoroughly review the whole matter before he was asked to look at the matter again. The Council took three years on their task but at last, in 1913, Lord Derby was able to speak of building a 'big' Masonic Hall in Manchester. 'It was something that ought to be done,' he said, and East Lancashire ought to be second to no other Provincial organisation in having a building worthy of their Province . . . ' £10,000 was estimated as the cost of the land required, and £15,000 would be needed for erecting and furnishing the premises.

The Masonic Hall, Bridge Street, Manchester.

The good news was given that the land was available and whilst it would need great efforts by the local brethren the PGM expressed the hope that they would not mind the Provincial Grand Lodge giving some financial assistance so that 'we may have a proper building for our purposes. The building will be built to accommodate 40 or 50 lodges in the vicinity', he continued, 'and, I hope, when finished, it will be a building second to none in the Masonic world.' Without any premonition at that date that an assassination in what is now Yugoslavia would alter things dramatically the Joint Secretaries to the General Committee for the building of the new Masonic Hall issued a circular letter. It put the facts for the project and the aims to be achieved very clearly.

They showed that of 68 lodges meeting in the area only 17 could meet at Cooper Street, 6 out of 13 RA Chapters and only half the other units in other orders. The site now chosen was that which had been occupied by the old Queen's Theatre in Bridge Street, itself the main throughfare between Manchester and Salford whilst also being in easy walking distance from all the principal stations used by those coming into the two cities. From the outset it was proposed to have not only the facility of rooms to help in governing the Province, but a strong basement for safe storage of lodge and other records, a masonic library and museum with reading room, temples and dining rooms, kitchens and serving areas and a general or smoking room where 'brethren may meet their Masonic friends for friendly intercourse'. The price, however, had now risen to £40,000. It was suggested that, taking into account the help that might be expected from other sources, the sum needed in balance could be met by each of the 4000 brethren in East Lancashire contributing £5 over the next two or three years. Bearing in mind the distinguished names that now adorn the various parts of the present building it is worth noting that the Chairman of the General Committee was a WBro J. B. Goulburn, PGD, Deputy PGM.

In 1914, with the war having broken out, the statement made by this Deputy PGM at the Stockport Town Hall, where Provincial Grand Lodge was being held, referred to the need to make haste more slowly and to use any delay as a chance to 'examine their plans more closely and to make a better building than possibly they might have had had they gone on as hastily.' It was now that the projected structure was referred to as the 'Temple' and that is the name which these Provincial headquarters bore until it reverted to being Freemasons' Hall from January 1988.

In 1919 the Province paid tribute to its war heroes when the Archdeacon of Manchester, the Ven Noel Aspinall, PPGCh, referred not only to those who died in battle but also to WBro Goulburn who died in November 1918. This latter brother did not even see the commencement of the building work above ground for this did not start until 1922 and it was only on 4 October, 1925 that the Foundation Stone was laid by electrical remote control whilst the members of the Province attended Lord Derby at the Free Trade Hall, a quarter of a mile away. The portrait of this long serving ruler of East Lancashire, who was PGM for just short of 50 years, now hangs proudly in the alcove behind the Master's chair in the Derby Lodge Room gracing the superb furnishings which were shortly to be made available for masonic use.

At last, on 24 October, 1929, HRH the Prince of Wales, KG, PGW, Provincial Grand Master for Surrey, dedicated the Temple, but the circumstances attendant upon this special day are particularly worthy of note.

The finished building at that time consisted of four suites of lodge and dining rooms. They were named Derby, Goulburn, Starkie (after the PGM, Col Le Gendre N. Starkie, 1870–99) and Sykes (the name of the Deputy PGM appointed in 1919 and who was to succeed Lord Derby in 1948). As there were three thousand ticket holders they were seated throughout the Temple with each lodge room arranged as if for its usual purpose, and official officers appointed to occupy the various chairs. Loud speakers—then a very recent innovation—were fitted in each room and connected with the central microphone in the Derby suite. As the lodge was opened in the three degrees there so, in silence, the same ceremony was conducted in each of the other rooms and all present could feel that they were part of the main ceremony.

The Prince of Wales passed the original foundation stone as he mounted the front steps and then unveiled and illuminated the commemorative tablet on the west wall of the central Memorial Hall which so impresses and inspires the newcomer even to this day. The tablet which he thus exposed for the first time reads as follows:

> This Hall enshrines the memory of all Freemasons from the province of East Lancashire who, of their Faith and valour, made the Supreme Sacrifice for King and Country during the years of War, MCMXIV–MCMXVIII.

Underneath that inscription there is a most moving one 'MCMXXXIX–MCMXLV' reminding us of even further sacrifices in the more recent conflict.

The Derby Suite is just one of many temples used. The portrait above the WM's chair is of Lord Derby.

The hall itself, as can be seen, is of the finest neo-classical design with three tall, fluted columns on both sides all supporting a bold but finely moulded architrave that runs all round this rectangular area. The roof above is of semi-circular shape and covered with a regular array of square recesses of which the central ones at the apex of the roof are filled with glass to give the maximum light during daytime. Entering the hall from the main foyer at the entrance one faces the plain white marble flooring and at the other end a flight of eight steps leading to the entrance doors of the Derby Suite.

Above this door is a decorated form of the Derby family arms and higher still, at the level of the architrave, there can be seen an iron balustrade, actually on the third floor, protecting those who can walk all round the outside of the barrel-vaulted ceiling to reach other lodge rooms and suites.

Plaques affixed to the walls of the Memorial Hall are in memory of Lord Derby, Sir Alan Sykes, and RWBro Frederick Towns, PGW, Deputy PGM, 1962–71. In the doorway leading to the hall is a bronze tablet bearing the names of three brethren who were awarded the Order of Service to Masonry—Bros Wm Horrocks, Canon Paton-Williams and Sir Frank Lord. The whole effect of this magnificent entrance structure is to induce at once the sense of dignity, awe and respect for those masons who encounter this worthy Provincial centre.

In addition to the suites of rooms which have already been mentioned the Temple at Bridge Street now contains three others. These are the Rhodes, the Towns and the Hewlett Suite. The first commemorates Sir Edward Rhodes who for over 30 years held high office in the Province and was then installed as PGM at 80 years of age and ruled for a further nine years. The second bears the name of one who was the father of the present PGM and who served as Assistant Provincial Grand Master and Deputy from 1947 to 1971 and was then accorded the special distinction of being made Past Grand Warden in the United Grand Lodge of England on the appointment of Sir Clyde Hewlett as Provincial Grand Master. The last, using what was meant to be a 'penthouse', is reserved for RArch.

The appointments of these various suites are fully consonant with the highest standards of craftsmanship in every sense. Anyone who has had the privilege, as has the author, of practising his masonry within their walls will have gained a sense of the dignity and high importance of the Craft from the mere quality of the carved panelling, the substantial furniture, the well calculated acoustics, the excellence of the seating—and above all the ample spaciousness of even the smaller lodge rooms. He will have sampled the adequate rehearsal rooms and, not least, he will have dined comfortably and well in a special and separate dining room which is attached to his lodge meeting place. It is thus that, whilst the dimensions and scope of this temple are so large there is, for those who use it, a remarkable sense of privacy and intimacy once a lodge has occupied its particular suite.

In terms of antiquity, a feature so well illustrated by other halls mentioned in this volume, it may well appear to the general visitor to Bridge Street that the modern, if solid, décor of the lodge rooms has vanquished the past. Apart from the display of some ancient warrants and some old banners during lodge meetings there is little else to convey the age and distinctiveness of so many lodges that meet here. It is to the museum on the third floor that the visitor needs to go in order to assure himself of the traditions and treasures that have come down to us from 250 years of masonry in this part of the country.

The imposing entrance and War Memorial Hall at Manchester.

It is, of course, impossible in the compass of these few pages to convey the richness and variety of the items that are kept here. A few examples will have to suffice.

In the four corners of the museum there have now been installed bracket showcases in which there are many examples of pre- and early post-Union aprons. The individuality and distinctiveness of these pieces of clothing is enhanced by the useful descriptions which have been attached to each frame and there is ample scope here for much masonic study. The arrangement and preservation of these local items is a tribute to the archivist.

In each of the delicate glass-fronted cases around the room there are displays of items connected with one degree or another. For those especially interested in the Mark and the Knightly Orders there are reminders here of the flourishing nature of these aspects of masonry in the late eighteenth and nineteenth century in this area. It is, for instance, only a year ago that an exhibition was mounted on these premises to mark the bicentenary of the Jerusalem Preceptory in Manchester. There is also a fine array of pottery with some special designs and verse, and some samples of early tracing boards, including the miniature set by Harris. Over the main fireplace is an interesting set of early nineteenth century jewels, one or two of them unique, but the most remarkable possession in the room is a framed copy of one of the earliest post-Reformation charges to freemasons in its original state. For those who have never realised the ancestors of the words read to a prospective Master by a Secretary here is a wonderful opportunity for them to do so. Few things in this museum so eloquently remind us of our past and the fact that a lodge at Warrington was the very first to be recorded as proof of Freemasonry's existence even in 1641.

Fascinating and intriguing as the museum is it has to be realised that this hall also contains a well-stocked masonic library. The full measure of its contents has yet to be discovered but even the most casual glance along the shelves of yet another elegant room with its lofty ceiling, white-painted, glass fronted cupboards and showcases reveals that this is not just another humdrum assemblage of material. It is fairly certain that a proper cataloguing will unearth some valuable research material for local students.

Together, then, with these two collections for help with masonic advancement, the Long Gallery that connects the two, the comfortable Members Lounge that lies immediately beneath this on the floor below, and the adequate suite of rooms that have been provided for the proper administration of so great a Province, this 'Temple' does indeed merit the term 'memorable'. To those familiar with it the impact of Freemasons' Hall in London will be that much less since here is a northern counterpart of no less quality. To those who come as visitors from elsewhere there will soon be a recognition that they are at the very hub of the second largest Province in our Constitution.

NEWCASTLE UPON TYNE

Maple Terrace Masonic Temple

ON THE AFTERNOON of 11 October, 1870, there was laid in Maple Street, Newcastle upon Tyne, the foundation stone of yet another masonic hall. Just what the occasion meant to those who gathered for that important local event is indicated by some words spoken when the trowel for laying the stone was handed over to the Chairman of the Company formed to undertake the work. Inviting Bro George Thompson to accept the trowel not merely for the work in hand but as a lasting memento of the occasion and as a tribute from those present the speaker continued: 'We all know the principles upon which our Order is founded but we are sometimes apt to forget one thing—our independence—and we should have here continued to forget if we had continued to rent a miserable room as we have lately done. There can be little doubt', he continued, 'that the Freemasons of Newcastle will be proud to possess a freehold of their own and that when this building is completed it will, I am sure, reflect not only great credit on the Craft but also on its chief promoter'. In the event George Thompson was the recipient not merely of a silver trowel (suitably inscribed) but also a mallet and square, in order that he might lay the stone in a business-like manner.

Bro Ludwig placed in a cavity of the stone a bottle containing all the coins of Victoria's reign together with copies of newspapers and other documents and on the stone being set in place Bro Foulsham 'offered up an impressive prayer'. In his closing remarks Bro Thompson pointed out that almost every large town in England now had a masonic hall whereas in this large and flourishing city of Newcastle the freemasons had had no such place to call their own. He alluded to the unsuccessful attempts which had been made by the Craft to obtain such a building over a fairly long period and stated that it was mainly the St Peter's No 481 and Northern Counties lodges which had taken the main initiative in this venture. It is therefore of great interest to note that the St Peter's Lodge still meets here in the hall along with six other Craft lodges, four Royal Arch chapters and two Mark lodges of which one is the Northumberland and Berwick-upon-Tweed Mark Lodge TI (Time Immemorial). Nor forgetting the Newcastle College of Societas Rosicruciana in Anglia, which has met in the Temple since 1890 and holds an extensive library of rare books and publications in many languages in the high-domed library on the first floor.

Bro Thompson went on to emphasize that when the hall was finished it would enable the masons to perform their rites and ceremonies 'in a quiet manner which would add to the solemnity of their proceedings' (which remark seems to imply volumes for the previous standards expected) and it is notable that he stressed the

The large kneeling stool and the magnificent pillars by the entrance are significant. The chairs used by the Wardens and Junior Deacon are also impressive.

fact that the accommodation would be ample and sufficient for the whole Province to meet in. It was clear that the plans which had been approved were meant from the start to give Newcastle masons a hall that was going to be much too large for any one unit to manage.

It was meant to be 18 months before the finished building could be dedicated but on May 23, 1872, a very large number of freemasons gathered for the occasion. It is hard today to imagine the scene for the area has changed so much and what today seems like an island structure in a sea of light industry must then have been a prestigious hall in a largely residential suburb. What is in fact so memorable about this meeting place is that its location is unexpected and its continuity as a temple is so remarkable. Outwardly its style is typically late-Victorian, being neo-Gothic and with much symbolic carving, but its impression is somewhat bleak being of stone. The surprise occurs when you mount the front steps, enter the hallway and shut out the late twentieth century Newcastle that initially greeted you.

At the hour appointed for the dedication ceremony nearly 200 masons had assembled in the building and this in itself begins to convey a sense of the hall's dimensions. The hall consists of two floors and a basement with various outbuildings and not only were the brethren able to sit in the spacious temple but most of them were also able to sit down to dinner in the basement dining room. In their original condition the premises must have been very impressive and have filled the

In the east of the temple is this fine stained glass window depicting masonic emblems.

local masons with a real sense of encouragement for the future. They were to be a trifle disappointed on this special day, however, for though they had expected the Rt Hon the Earl Percy, PGM of Northumberland, to preside they received a letter in the early afternoon expressing his lordship's regret that due to an indisposition he could not join them as planned and that his Deputy, Maving Lonsdale Cockcroft, Esq, would carry out the ceremony supported by Lord James Murray, representative of the Grand Lodge of Scotland at the Grand Lodge of England.

The building today has suffered not a little from the passage of time and it was quite possible, a decade ago, when extensive dry rot was discovered, that the hall might have come to its natural end. Some lodges that met there decided that they could not face the challenge that was involved in getting the hall back into effective working order and left, but due not least to the work of many of the members of the remaining lodges and chapters who gave their *free time*, energies and craftsmanship, and also gave full support to the money raising activities of the 'Restoration Fund Committee', they won the battle.

Full credit should be given to lodges 481, 2568, 3187, 5287, 6049 and 6317, and chapters 418, 3892, 4017, 6049 who remained faithful to their trust, and had the remedial treatment carried out and paid for and today a most distinctive masonic meeting place has been maintained free of debt. As those who make the effort to penetrate the surroundings and the stairway to the first floor will soon discover there is here a temple that it would have been a tragedy to lose. The keeping of Maple Terrace hall is a lesson which might well have been learned by several other masons elsewhere whose traditional homes have been allowed to slip into oblivion.

Adjoining the main lodge room there is ample provision for the sort of numbers that were in fact accommodated at the opening ceremony. There are robing and sitting rooms as well as a satisfactory Tyler's room and recent decoration and renovation have again begun to update what could otherwise be simply an old-fashioned Victorian building. Yet it is the temple which is the real treasure of the site and even though the staircase is wide and the outer rooms sizeable the effect of entering the main hall is still a shock.

The room is 46 feet long by 24 feet across and well over 20 feet high. The lofty room is formed of typical wrought iron, moulded braces and ribs and recent re-painting has attempted to bring out the features of its century-old construction. What most immediately strikes the person entering are two huge pillars crowned with nets and pomegranates but without any kind of globes. The Inner Guard sits just to the right of the pillars against the west wall and is thus well positioned to scrutinise any entrant as well as receive candidates. To the left of the pillars is the organ which has before it a large smooth ashlar.

Looking a little further into the lodge room we now note that in the western half of the floor area there is a rectangle of chequered pavement with another and smaller smooth ashlar at its north east, and a comparable rough ashlar at its south east corner. There is clearly no attempt to make the pavement cover the whole lodge and one is strongly reminded of how a similar ratio of the floor being marked was probably the origin of the early tracing cloths or boards. To the west of this 'pavement' is a wide kneeling stool and behind that, and against the centre of the west wall, sits the SW in what looks like the original chair and pedestal.

The next point of interest is a central pedestal or altar placed just in front of the east side of the 'pavement' with a VSL and its own stool before it. It is here that obligations are taken, with the WM descending from the east to carry out this duty. We are here in direct link with those American lodges of today which have still retained this ancient practice, and as we see in at least one other hall in this series in England. The sight which greets an initiate when his blindfold is removed is what should now occupy our attention.

Across the whole length of the lower part of the east wall there is a very beautiful carved arcade of wooden tracery. At the time of its creation it was a new and most attractive feature in masonic architecture and was obviously intended to convey a sense of ecclesiastical grandeur. This is further emphasised by the fact that the screen is divided up into stalls and the seats beneath are wonderfully carved chairs, a tribute to master craftsmen of the late eighteenth century, the WM's chair in particular being most impressive.

The WM's chair and pedestal are placed under a more prominent crocketed canopy and he has to his left, when sitting, the Treasurer's desk in solid mahogany, and the Secretary with a similar desk to his right. Before both of these officers stands a pillar with a white globe which is lit up during meetings. The total effect is complete.

The screen at the east is not simply there for decoration. It was provided as the base for a set of four large lancet windows which are filled with masonic symbols, and also as the frame for another set of transparencies which are lit up at night by illumination from behind the screen.

At the apex of the window space is a quatrefoil which displays an All Seeing Eye within a halo of light and surrounded by the circle, representing eternity. In a medallion below this there is a star of brilliant cut glass on an azure ground and the aperture beneath this star reveals the masonic arms with motto and supporters. It is below this and above the screen that we have the amazing array of forms and figures that must impress by having the light through them in the daytime and by being also illuminated at night. The arrangement of the designs is as follows:

1. Terrestrial globe	Sun	Moon & Stars	Celestial globe
2. The Bible (*Truth*)	Justice with scales	Dove of Peace	Beehive (*industry*)
3. Hiram Abiff (*with plan*)	Solomon (*with Temple model*)	Hiram of Tyre (*with sceptre*)	Moses (*with 10 commandments*)
4. Eagle (*Faith*)	Anchor (*Hope*)	Heart (*Charity*)	Clasped Hands (*Brotherly Love*)

It can be well imagined what a remarkable effect such a display can have not only upon the casual visitor but even more upon those who come to light for the first time in this temple. It is an arrangement which does not have its like anywhere and it is, for this reason alone, a memorable feature of masonic meeting places. One can only rejoice that it was the determination of recent freemasons which has prevented such an unusual arrangement being lost to masonry in general and the north-east in particular. It is all the more remarkable in that from the outside of this building one could never guess at what was offered within.

The future of this place may seem more secure now that attempts have been made to ensure its structural soundness. It is for that reason that attempts to develop the premises and perhaps fully restore the once elegant clubroom on the top floor might be attempted. What is certain is that the present masons at Maple Terrace know what a heritage they have. For the author it has been a personal delight to find such a hall; for others it may well be a fresh delight to know about.

The Worshipful Master's pedestal is on a raised dais and has an imposing view over the temple.

SUNDERLAND

The Oldest Lodge Room

SUNDERLAND IS NOT the prettiest of places and there are some sections of the town which might be described as positively decayed. It is in one of those districts, down by the docks, that you come across what looks like the exterior of an old warehouse. The one remaining façade which was to give the building some indication of its masonic purpose has now been almost wholly smoothed over with re-plastering and so it is only the interior which loudly proclaims its use by the Antient Craft.

The Phoenix Lodge, which is so intimately linked with this hall, was constituted in 1755. At that time and for some years afterwards it met in local inns and taverns and was even known at one stage as 'The Lodge at the Golden Lion '. Yet as early as 1763 Capt George Thompson, who was Master of the Phoenix Lodge for several years, conceived the idea of divorcing Freemasonry from meeting in such public places and having a more private and appropriate environment.

Early in 1764 he secured a site in Vine Street from a Jonathan Burleigh but as this was insufficient to meet his requirements he had to wait until he could purchase additional land in 1775. Indeed, had Thompson been able to proceed with his plans in 1764 this Sunderland project would have been the first building in England erected solely for masonic purposes. The site for Freemasons Hall in Great Queen Street, London, was, it should be remembered, only purchased in the November of 1774.

With this opening of the lodge in the Vine Street hall the membership increased dramatically but just after the death of Capt Thompson in 1782 the hall was severely damaged by fire and everything was lost. It remained derelict until 1793, was then partially rebuilt and let for various purposes before being demolished in January 1937.

Until that time it was generally believed that the present Hall in Queen Street East was erected on the site of the former one and the Phoenix Lodge History of 1906 mentions it as a matter beyond dispute. However, the able researches of William Waples, a notable and local masonic scholar, showed that the two buildings were about a quarter of a mile apart. What had happened, he revealed, was that in December 1783 some 'Gentlemen of the Committee' were appointed to consider building a new hall which should be as near as possible an exact replica of that which had been burnt down.

Under the able leadership of the Worshipful Master, Dr Tipping Brown, MD, the work was done with speed and efficiency. The foundation stone was laid as early as 5 April, 1784 and the final dedication ceremony exactly one year later. The

Above: *The tops of the three principal officers chairs are richly decorated. The Master's displays the coat of arms of the 'Tower of the Lodge' whilst the Wardens show the sun and moon. These chairs were purchased in 1784 and are possibly the oldest still used in a masonic lodge.* Below: *The Senior Wardens' pedestal with organ gallery above.*

total cost of the project was £600 of which £360 was raised by the brethren in £20 shares and the remainder in donations. It is believed that whilst the interior design of the present hall is identical with Vine Street the exterior architecture is not. In this latter regard William Waples concluded that Vine Street was superior in every way and that the present Queen Street hall was but a passable imitation. Over the years, of course, some alterations and additions have been necessarily made to create the present premises. It is still probably the oldest, continuously occupied, masonic private premises in the country. As such it is indeed memorable.

Anyone who now enters the somewhat extended premises will soon be aware of the antiquity of what he encounters. The present ancillary rooms, erected from neighbouring houses which have been aquired, have already assumed that sense of age and dignity which particularly assails the visitor as he passes through the door of the original lodge room. This room has not been altogether left untouched by history. The original entrance was in the west, was then moved to the east, and the present doorway in the north-west only dates from 1921. Nonetheless there remains much of historical interest that distinguishes this old site from the most modern halls today.

In the centre of the ceiling is a Blazing Star enclosing the letter 'G' and seven stars within a triangle. This is said to measure 15 feet across and is an exact copy of that in the first Vine Street hall. The long upholstered benches also follow the Vine Street pattern.

On the north side are two beautiful ornamental "Adam" fireplaces, both of which were used for coal fires until 1926. It was between these two features that there once hung the original Phoenix banner in navy blue silk but early in the Second World War it was taken down to the cellar and there rapidly deteriorated. A lesson surely to any others who have old banners and wonder what to do with them! Something of what that banner looked like is still remembered by the Phoenix painting in the outside corridor, a representation of which is still preserved on the present Phoenix Lodge summons.

On this north wall you can see the very unusual tracing boards which were, of course, once placed over a large area of the lodge floor. They date from either 1811 or 1815 and certainly point to a pre-Union type of Masonry. They are not currently used for instruction purposes and since their restoration by cleaning in 1955 (the Lodge's Bicentenary) they have continued to be the subject of much investigation and speculation.

On the mantelpiece in the north east is an ancient brass dish looking very much like a miniature frying pan, which was used for collecting Alms and not least for presenting to a candidate at that part of the lodge room. It is believed that this was one of the few objects that was saved from the Vine Street fire. On the same mantelpiece is a Tot of Rum jug in pewter. It bears the number 146 and the initials 'G. R.' and was, I am told, one of several that were not unnaturally used in a lodge that had many seafaring men in its membership.

The dominating feature at the west end of the room is the gallery with the organ, which was built in 6 weeks in 1784–5 by a Mr Donaldson. It then cost £50. A gap in the right hand side of the organ gallery accommodated a ladder which led to the organ seat but since 1922 the whereabouts of that feature have not been known.

The Dais at the east end is an exact replica of that in the Vine Street hall and the pedestal and altar both date from 1785. Until 1947 there were also two Spheres,

Above: *The original but unfinished entrance facade*. Below: *The east view of the temple which has a separate pedestal for the VSL.*

celestial and terrestrial, situated on this Dais but again, through unfortunate neglect, both were broken beyond repair. Above the Master's Chair is seen the symbol of the Rising Sun and this is balanced around the room by the Crescent Moon above the Senior Warden's Chair in the west and the Meridian Sun in all its splendour above the Junior Warden's place in the south. These symbols, like the replicas of them on the officers' chairs, were carved and gilded by Bro Pears of Newcastle who had also been responsible for the originals in Vine Street. It is thus known that he gave to this hall the exact copies of his earlier work. The carving and gilding then cost £30 and it is noteworthy that no restoration work has been carried out since then.

The officers' chairs are very old and truly magnificent. They are possibly as old as any used in any Masonic lodge anywhere and the minutes of the 'Gentlemen of the Committee' record that they were purchased in 1784.

The Master's Chair is worthy of close examination and the vine decoration on it would suggest an origin connected with early Christian masonry. As a certain St John's Lodge was selling up its effects in Newcastle at the very time when these chairs were purchased it is not unlikely that the 'vine' in St John's Gospel is here the one referred to. Above the Chair is the 'Tower of the Lodge' which was the Coat of Arms placed there by the special direction of the 'Gentlemen'. It was intended to perpetuate the Badge of the Lodge from that early date. The gilding on this chair has never been restored and so it may well be 200 years or more since it was done. The Wardens' chairs match that of the Master and thus give a remarkable sense of unity and antiquity to the whole room.

Even so the latticed carved chairs of the Treasurer and Secretary are probably more ancient than the ones we have just noticed. One expert has suggested that they may be Chippendale and along with those of the matching Deacons and Past Masters chairs appear to have been made for a Masons lodge. They fit this temple perfectly and the pedestals with round tray tops which accompany the Deacons chairs add yet another embellishment to this truly distinctive temple. The Wardens' columns certainly have the appearance of being, as is believed, another relic of the burnt out Vine Street home from which they may have come.

Another item of historic interest is the floorcloth of the Royal Arch which was used when this degree was practiced under the Craft warrant, sometime around 1772. In 1797 the floorcloth was loaned to the then new Strict Benevolence Chapter formed by members of the Phoenix and Palatine old Royal Arches. That chapter was to cease work in 1816 but it is worth remarking that the floorcloth is still used on loan by the Royal Arch bodies meeting in this ancient hall and they thus share in a history that far outstrips their own.

Whatever one's first impressions of the district may be this is a piece of masonic memorabilia not to be missed by any who travel this way.

WAKEFIELD

The Hall on the Old Rectory Site

WHILST IT IS well known that Henry VIII was responsible for emptying and even destroying the monasteries of his day it is not so often remembered that he also appointed John Leland, his chaplain and librarian, to make a journey round the land to record the manuscripts, documents and buildings of those religious houses in the period before their dissolution was considered. No doubt the one act assisted the other but in approaching the story of the Masonic Hall at Wakefield it is worth noting that prior to the erection of the present building the Wakefield Lodge, which was formed in 1844 and first met in Thornhill Street, resolved in 1853 to move to the Rectory House which was mentioned by John Leland in his tour of 1538. The property had been so named, therefore, for at least three centuries, though mention of an appropriation of the property in 1348 suggests that 500 years would be more accurate.

The house was pleasantly situated and was fenced in by iron railings. It had usually been approached by 'Vicar's Lane' but to permit easier access to the recently established Borough Market (still vigorously alive today) a portion of the Rectory was dismantled and a new street was formed and given the name of the Earl of Zetland, who was then MW Grand Master of England. It is for this reason that the present hall stands in Zetland Street.

At the lodge of Emergency held on 26 August, 1853 a committee of Wakefield Lodge was appointed to purchase the property and devise the 'best means of raising the money' for that end. The purchase price was £300, of which £24 was contributed from lodge funds and the remaining amount was raised by shares at £10 each. A further sum was spent in adapting the premises for the better service of the lodge as well as on furnishings and decoration. It was to be the lodge's home for 27 years.

Even the remaining portion of the original two-storied, three-gabled house that the lodge took over was so roomy and convenient—it had wrought stone doorways and fireplaces, with diamond-shaped mullioned windows and solid wooden beams—that within a few years the Wakefield Lodge and Chapter had been joined by other local masonic bodies. The Lodge of Unanimity had been warranted in 1766 and, after being in the George and Crown tavern for nearly 30 years, it moved to the Bull for another 50 years and then began to decline. Some of the Wakefield Lodge members assisted its recovery and with its residence alongside the younger lodge at Zetland Street it began to regain its status as the mother lodge of the area.

The brethren of Sincerity Lodge No 1019, founded in 1864, also took up residence in the old Rectory House premises, as well as the chapters of these lodges and a Mark lodge removed from Morley. It was the growing popularity and use made of these rooms which naturally gave rise to the first queries about its permanent viability. By 1879 a circular letter to all members there expressed the concerns that were surfacing: 'The lodge and refreshment rooms are small and ill ventilated; the subsidiary rooms are insufficient; and the kitchen arrangements are very inconvenient and defective; whilst the age and consequent decay of the building entail a large annual outlay to keep the fabric in repair'. It was a common and yet happy reflection on the growth of the Craft. Certainly the problems must have been acute for the action taken was prompt and effective.

By 22 April, 1879, it was decided to demolish the Rectory. On 15 July a Committee was appointed and by 28 February, 1880, the project was launched with the last meeting taking place in 13 April.

When the Rectory House was demolished for the building of the new Masonic Hall in 1880, one cellar of the Rectory House was so situated that it lay under the proposed new road 'Zetland Street'. However, that cellar was left untouched and the new road built over it. For some reason it was connected by a doorway to the new hall. It is still there but boarded up. A decade or more ago two brethren removed the boarding and explored the old cellar. It extended some twenty feet from the wall of the hall to the other side of the new road where it had been roughly blocked off by stone and earth. Its paved flooring and vaulted tiles bearing masonic emblems were gathered and a few rotted balusters similar to those of the hall stairway already referred to were lying about.

The new foundation stone was laid on 26 May, with the first meeting in the new premises on 9 November. Even though the dedication was not until 1883 it showed how Yorkshire men can get a job done, and with what expedition they avoided any undue interruption to their masonic programme.

The laying of the foundation stone and its attendant festivities has been delightfully told by WBro R. E. Midgley and certainly some of his narrative helps to show how fully such a beginning was linked with the life of the town. Queen Victoria was on the throne and Gladstone was Prime Minister when, on that day in 1880, 'the day had started with overcast skies and the threat of rain . . . '

'There was, as usual, bustle about the city and curiosity at the number of carriages to be seen in the streets, particularly in the vicinity of the Town Hall' during the morning. 'The activity, however, which was in fact centred on the Music Saloon, now the city museum, had actually subsided by about 1:00 p.m.'

'Inside the Music Saloon it was a different and unusual story, for 150 freemasons in full regalia had assembled and . . . a lodge meeting had been opened in the three degrees and received its guest of honour who had only recently arrived . . . ' The Provincial Grand Master, Sir Henry Edwards, had been expected but the Deputy PGM, Thomas William Tew, a banker from Pontefract with business interests in Wakefield, was here in place of the ailing Sir Henry.

'The public attention was soon to be again attracted by the masons emerging from the Music Saloon in masonic clothing with bright and glistening paraphenalia carrying banners and emblems'. The procession was headed by the Wakefield Military Band, and Mr Clarkson, the Chief Constable and an 'efficient staff of police to prevent any confusion or disorder'. 'By a devious route the procession

The dining room officer's chairs, previously of Lodge of Unanimity, have inlaid motifs on the top of the backs. Below left: *The Warrant of Wakefield Lodge dated 1844 with unusual frame and ladder.* Below right: *The Senior Wardens' chair is Jacobean whilst the 'Three Legs' support the ashlar.*

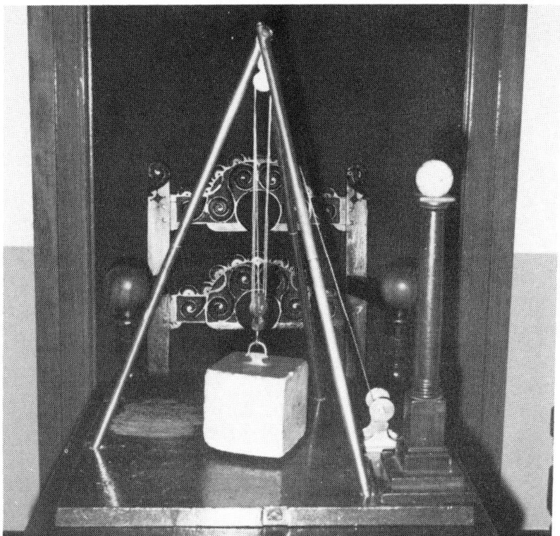

eventually arrived in Zetland Street and halted in front of a large dais, having collected some 27 members of the choir of Pontefract Parish Church along the way'. The platform party took their places, with the ladies having a vantage point from the playground of the nearby Parish Church School. Rain was very much feared but "as the choir sang the 100th Psalm to the tune "The Old Hundredth" a dramatic change took place and soon the sun was shining brightly showing off the emblems of the brethren'.

'The Vicar of Sheffield, the Provincial Grand Chaplain, then read the 127th Psalm' and after a glass bottle containing lists of the three lodges' members, the ceremony's programme, the site plans and newspapers of the day had been placed in the same cavity the foundation stone was solemnly laid by Bro Tew. 'At each of the three stops of the ceremony the choir sang a verse of the beautiful masonic ode "Round the Spot" by Dr Spark of Leeds . . .' and following the use of the corn, wine and oil, "The Vicar of Horsforth, a past Grand Master (*sic*), offered prayer, after which the acolyte, though having some difficulty in producing a flame, scattered incense over and around the stone as a symbol of purity'.

In his closing remarks at the site Bro Tew remarked: 'On the excellency of Freemasonry I feel that little debate is necessary . . . Its three pillars are wisdom, strength and reality, symbolic of faith, hope and mercy . . . and though the walls of this material edifice must one day succumb to time I express the hope that it may have administered to increase the knowledge of the wonderful works of the Almighty Creator and the happiness of the brethren who will have entered its portals'. The choir closed with 'Hail Masonry Divine' and the leading of the National Anthem, and then went to be dined at the Royal Hotel at Bro Tew's expense whilst the heavens opened and the rain at last arrived.

It is then into this hall, opened with so much prayer and planning, that we can now enter. The street may not be quite so prestigious today as it was in 1880 but the blue doorway with its imposing pediment, containing a shield and the square and compasses surrounded by the folds of cornucopia, distinguishes the structure from its featureless neighbours. On entering one immediately senses the cosiness and intimacy of this meeting-place, now more than a century old, and the first sense of the past comes as you pass through a door to the right of the hallway and see the main chairs at the dining table. This is a long table of $1\frac{3}{4}$ inch thick chestnut; it is only plank, 24 ft long and 30 inches wide, supported on eight turned legs. It is authoritatively recorded as having been reduced in length by $4\frac{1}{2}$ ft to suit the length of the room, and is disputed to have come from the old Rectory House. The three mahogany armchairs, with wide leather seats and tall pillared backs, were made for Lodge of Unanimity No 154 in 1766 at a cost of £8 9s 6d for the lot. They are worthy of any lodge room and the more so as they are especially noteworthy in having a circular wooden medallion at the apex of each backrest. That for the Junior Warden is a sun in full glory; that for the Senior Warden a golden crescent moon with human features facing to the left as you look at it; and that for the Worshipful Master bears a beehive with bees, thus declaring the main source of labour in the lodge and proclaiming the pre-Union nature of the furniture. If one wonders why these lovely chairs are only used at the after-proceedings the answer is provided by a report of the new Building Committee in 1881. They said:

> ... much commendation has been expressed regarding the appearance and general arrangements of the building, and also respecting the admirable proportions and good acoustic properties of the principal rooms. It has been felt, however, that much is needed to be done to give the Lodge such an air of completeness as will be conducive not only to the efficiency of the working but also to the comfort and enjoyment of the Brethren. The furniture, which was not unsuitable or insufficient for the old Lodge, is found to be inadequate and ill-adapted for the new Building, and it is absolutely necessary that new carpets, curtains, etc. should be at once provided. It is estimated that not less than £250 will be required to furnish the Lodge in an appropriate and substantial manner.

Those who had not already made a donation were now asked to offer a subscription so that: 'visiting Brethren may with pride be introduced within its walls, and in the future it will form a fitting memorial to the Masonic spirit of the present day'.

The Wakefield Lodge faithfully discharged that duty for nearly 70 years until the present Wakefield Masonic Hall Company was set up to buy and administer the premises. It was actually registered on 10 May, 1947.

As we pass upstairs from the hallway it is worth realising that the balusters of the oak staircase were those which were transferred from the old Rectory House and we are thus always held in bond with the masons who used this approach to the lodge room long before the present building. It might even be that we are mounting the stairs which in part have been in place on this site as long as as the ceiling, uncovered in the Rectory House demolition, that bore the date 1348. Both the domestic and masonic past are here united.

That the sums of £100 each donated by the lodges of Unanimity and Sincerity were well applied is clear as soon as you enter the main temple of Zetland Street. Though by no means large it is a well proportioned room that is almost a double cube, with lofty ceiling and a Glory painted at its centre. The prevailing colours are white, blues and light brown woodwork and the whole room has a sense of very great care and attention. The entrance door itself is picked out in brown and blue, with the words *AUDI . VIDE . TACE* above the door itself and between the carved ends of the pediment a graceful square and compasses.

The west, south and north walls are white with a lower band of blue but the east end is panelled to half its height and then covered with a band of blue on which are the gold-lettered words—"Behold, how good and pleasant a thing it is for brethren to dwell together in Unity." (*Psalm* 133). Around the whole room and above the walls is a dado of small linked arches and then another frieze of blue below the ceiling mouldings. This frieze carries the emblems of a griffin at each corner and in between a level, square, a Lorraine cross, the joined square and compasses, a triangle and then another griffin. The blue ceiling amply covers the whole room with a sense of calm and spaciousness.

Yet it is the main chairs and their canopies, together with their pillars, that rightly capture the lasting attention of the visitor.

In the middle of the east wall is a curved recess hung with three lengths of crimson, blue and green curtain. Above them, and on the pale blue surface of the semi-dome of the apse is a delicate rising sun whose gentle rays merge imperceptibly, as in reality, into the blue 'atmosphere' around. These features are encased in

Views of the lodge furniture with painted motifs.

a most exquisite oak casing that stretches up to the dado above. On the front of the case and across the square pediment is a blue scroll with the words in gold—'How wonderful are thy works' between which appears an all-seeing eye. Below this and on the curved woodwork that shapes to the curve of the semi-dome there are further fine decorations of the corn, acacia, ankh (or scared Egyptian symbol of life), the square and compasses, the pentagram and drops of water. Even more striking are the two fine pillars that seem to support this upper frame but in fact stand slightly to the fore of the plain wood which bears it. These pillars are turquoise green in shade, with pomegranate leaves at their head and above these are two black-based globes. The Master's well-carved chair is of very black wood and is carved with no date, though of seventeenth century style, but is almost lost within this admirable setting.

In addition, and reproduced at the Wardens' places, there is a slender pure white pillar of Greek style, carrying an opaque white glass bowl at its head, and on the front face of the tall square base a black roundel showing an L. On those of similar size and design for the wardens a level and plumbline are displayed. These pillars are respectively of the Ionic Order for the Master, Doric Order for the SW, and Corinthian Order for the JW and the three identical mahogany pedestals of the Master and Wardens are c1820.

The Wardens' chairs, which have similar rich black woodwork and decoration, are ridgebacks with ball-topped arms and each of them is set under a canopy of less prominence than that of the Master but each with its appropriate painted scene in the projected panel above a crimson backdrop. For the Senior Warden a setting sun is shown to the right of the panel with a vague outline of the moon in the top left corner. For the Junior Warden there is a 'burning' sun at the top edge of the panel suggesting the warm midday.

This room is further adorned with banners and ancient, well-framed warrants. The oldest banners of Unanimity and Sincerity hang in the north-east corner, whilst in the south-east are those of more modern lodges and that of the Integrity Mark Lodge. The latest edition, in the south-west, is that of the Richard Linnecar Lodge and was presented in March 1897 to commemorate the 40th anniversary of the lodge's consecration. The banner displays Richard Linnecar sitting, as in a contemporary portrait, in the 'Beehive' Master's chair that we saw in the dining room. He was the first Secretary of the Lodge of Unanimity, having been initiated in Gibraltar in 1743. The original picture of Linnecar, here reproduced, was painted in 1787 by Henry Singleton, RA, for and by the lodge. As Linnecar, with Craft collar and RA sash, was also Master of Unanimity for 26 years (!) it is only right that he should be shown occupying the chair that was truly his. Immediately below the new banner is the warrant of the new Richard Linnecar Lodge.

The most impressive of the other warrants in the room is that which hangs on the wall behind the Secretary's table. It is that of the Wakefield Lodge No 495, which had built the hall, and it is framed twice—once around the actual warrant, and that frame set on a crimson background and framed once more in a substantial 'pillared' frame of mahogany. The first frame is worth careful preservation for it is painted with gold leaf, has four medallions with fleur de lis at the corners, a frieze pattern of two pairs of crossed square and compasses with level and plumbline on each side, a painted glory with the all-seeing eye in the the top side centre and in the middle of the bottom edge a pedestal with an open VSL and a ladder of nine rungs reaching up the glass face of the warrant itself. Nor is this all! Above the 'all-seeing eye' is another open VSL with two flanges at its sides bearing yet more squares and compasses, and, surmounting the open book, a gold Pentagram in the form of a star that stands out sharply against the white north wall. Of such importance did our forefathers think their warrant to be that it received treatment that still enhances it today. They placed it in the centre of the north wall above a massive grey-green mottled marble fireplace with was removed only some thirty years ago to give more seating room. The other original warrant on the south wall, behind the Secretary and to his left, is equally important, being that of the Lodge of Unanimity No 154, the third oldest lodge in the West Riding; it is special because it is illuminated with stylized masonic emblems added to the warrant by Michael Devon, a clerk in the then Grand Secretary's office. A small number of similarly illuminated warrants still exist but those bearing Devon's signature, as Unanimity's does, are very rare. Beside that 1766 warrant hang the lodge's centenary and bi-centenary warrants. Feasting our eyes on these as on so much else that adorns this much-loved place, we may rightly claim that Wakefield's masonic home is memorable indeed. The fact that this hall has already produced two Past Masters of Quatuor Coronati Lodge, Bros. Rylands and Read shows the service that this centre has given to the past and future history of the Craft.

WARRINGTON

The Hall in Elias Ashmole Country

In many of the halls which have been described in this and the two companion volumes we have remarked on the variety of positions for the two great pillars of Boaz and Jachin. Some have stood at the east end, some at the west end and some half-way down the lodge. Others have been placed just inside the entrance door of the temple and some just outside the door, whilst yet others have been found at the entrance of the foyer or corridor leading to the lodge room door. All of them without exception have been *inside* the hall premises even if their precise location has been so varied.

No-one passing the Masonic Hall at Warrington can be left in any doubt about the nature of the building they see. Here the two great pillars stretch up their vast height, their carved capitals and the globes above them, *outside* the hall's main entrance. There is no hesitation here. The meaning of what 'the uninstructed and popular world' may gaze upon is not made plain but it must be obvious to anyone in the street that these unavoidable decorations of the doorway carry special significance for the men who pass in and out of this place.

Certainly the pillars add considerably to the character of what is otherwise a rather matter-of-fact exterior for quite a modern building. Freemasonry in this part of the world however is not in the least modern for it was here in the environs of this present busy town that we have evidence of the initiation of Elias Ashmole on 16 October, 1646, as the first recorded candidate in English speculative masonry. Of course those who were present, and who in part received him into their lodge, must also have been candidates at an even earlier stage but of their beginnings we have no present record. As far as Warrington masons are concerned they are walking on a part of England that has enviable and irreproducible Craft connections. The hall which serves this ancient town has enough reminders of a long past to bolster that conviction.

The first recorded lodge in Warrington, following the historic initiation of Ashmole, was founded there in 1755 and was numbered No 40 on the register of the Antients Grand Lodge. It was constituted on August 20th to meet at the Cock Inn, Bridge Street, but sadly lasted only a twelvemonth though it was 1791 before its warrant was sold to another lodge that was to meet in Quebec, Canada! Its successor was to be much more sturdy, warranted as No 352 on the Register of the premier, or Moderns, Grand Lodge and beginning in 1765. At first it had no name but at last the Grand Lodge, in 1806, gave permission for it to be called the Lodge of Lights. It is with this famous lodge that Warrington's masonry really begins.

Left: *The entrance to Warrington Masonic Hall.* Below: *The original 'Lodge of Lights' Geneva Bible.*

The Master's chair in the main temple, one of a set of three for the officers.

Above: *A pre-Union decorated plate.*

Right: *An early Royal Arch jewel.*

Below and right: *The two Wardens' chairs with carved back panels.*

Its first meeting place was at the Golden Fleece Inn in Buttermarket Street but within four years it had moved to Lingham's Coffee House in Horsemarket Street. Subsequently it migrated to the Woolpack and the Swan before again resuming life at the Golden Fleece in 1797, with the number 198. This kind of 'wandering' continued, as in so many other places which have been mentioned in these pages, until, after using the Wagon and Horses, Bear's Paw, Nagg's Head and The Bull, it was more soberly established in the old Officers' Mess of the Lancashire Militia in Bold Street. The date was now 1893. It stayed there for nearly 30 years and then, from 1921 until 1932, it lodged at the Lion Hotel in Bridge Street.

That was the last of its 'temporary' homes for in the latter year this ancient lodge joined with six others (Friendship, Charity, Rectitude, Ashmole, St Austin and St Oswald) and the foundations were at last laid for the present building in Winmarleigh Street. The plot was bought for £675 and this was offset by each lodge member contributing 3 guineas, some buying an armchair for £0 10s 0d and others a dining chair for five shillings.

The architects were the firm of Messrs Warburton & Co. and only masonic builders were approached for tenders. The land was bought in March 1932 and by April, Fairclough the builder, had been granted the contract at a first figure of £8200 which subsequently rose to £9765. In July the Chairman, H. Hope Evans of Friendship Lodge, was requested by the Committee to approach Lord Derby for the laying of the foundation stone and though this was at first agreed by the PGM it eventually turned out that he was unable to be present and the Deputy Provincial Grand Master, A. Forster PGD came in his place. The event took place on 22 September of the same year. It is worth noting that those attending prepared themselves in the nearby Church or Patten Hall. The dedication of the building took place on 22 November, 1933.

It was a most handsome structure by the standards of the time with two lodge rooms, a ballroom cum banqueting room, a smaller dining room, a lounge with bar, and a modern kitchen. What strikes a fresh visitor is the compactness of the site and the excellent use made of every part of the area, not least its centrally placed and branching staircase leading to the landings above from which the meeting rooms are reached.

Mounting the stairs, in fact, also reminds the visitor of the antiquity of much that is associated with local lodges. In two display cases there are numerous items that will catch the eye of anyone interested in our masonic past. Pieces of masonic glass with emblems not only of the Craft and Royal Arch but of Knight Templar, Knight Kadosh and the Mark. There are two ancient Royal Arch jewels attached to original neck ribbons—the one showing two columns linked by a stepped base, with a circle between enclosing two interlaced triangles and the sun in glory at the centre: whilst the other is the same motif without the flanking columns. There is also a large leather-bound Bible of the Geneva edition from the sixteenth century, with a tooled cover showing a square and compasses in the FC position but bearing the words 'Warrington Lodge' and that was the older name of the Lodge of Lights. The VSL shows clear use of having been much used and bears the tell-tale markings on pages associated with Ruth, St John and Amos—page choices that were associated with the different degrees and the Royal Arch. There is also a brass ballot box of uncommon design, and a charity collecting box that bears the words 'Work while ye may'. Already the visitor can sense the aura of a long-standing Freemasonry around this site and will be expecting other treasures to appear. He is not to be disappointed.

Mention was made earlier of the 'reminders' of the past and it will come as no surprise to learn that the minute books of the 'Lodge of Lights' are extant here from 1790 to the present day. The only disappointment for the lodge members is that they start so late! Herein we learn of how the form of the lodge was indeed drawn in chalk and charcoal by the Tyler but erased by the latest initiate. Initiation trousers are recorded as having been bought for one guinea, whilst the Master had first a three-cornered hat and later a silk one which was only removed for prayers.

The deacon's jewel that is still worn today is a Mercury bearing the caduceus—a staff interwoven with a serpent. These are pre-Union jewels and the collar jewels of the Master and his wardens are also original, of white metal with texts from the New Testament engraved on the back.

Moreover, in the smaller upstairs lodge room the original chairs of the Master and Wardens of the Lodge of Lights can also be seen. They are Chippendale and were made for the lodge in 1765. Similar to the pierced jewels of the period the chairs have open fretwork for their backs. These display the appropriate working tools, including the level and plumbline, and the Bible for the two Wardens' chairs but with the Master's chair bearing the armorial device of a chevron between three castles, the arms granted to the 'Hole Crafte and Fellowship of Masons' in 1472. The WM's chair also bears two gilded lozenges, one depicting the face of the sun with its spreading rays and the other a representation of the emergent moon.

The Wardens' chairs have three lozenges apiece and these are similarly and yet differently adorned. The centre one for the Senior Warden bears a classical porch having a domed roof, 4 pillars and 3 steps. Another of them shows a heavy setting maul and chisel whilst the design on the third has been so worn with use that it is not today distinguishable. The Junior Warden's chair has suffered less and displays three very distinctive arrangements—the centre lozenge has the face of a clock showing 12:30 (High Time, or after high noon), the one on the left shows the square on the hypotenuse of the right-angled triangle, whilst the remaining lozenge reveals a rough and smooth ashlar with a 24 in rule.

It is worth mentioning, as we look at these distinguished chairs, that they must have assisted at some fascinating events. Promotion to and through them was often rapid like that of Bro W. Titterington who was initiated on 26 August, 1822, Passed 30 September, Raised 28 October and became Junior Warden 25 November. That same night he 'passed the Chair' (presumably to let him join the Chapter) and in December 1823 he was Senior Warden, becoming Master in 1825. The 'Passing the Chair' ceremony was continued until 1855.

The lodge boasts a special Centenary Jewel, a possession which is only shared by one other Lancashire lodge, No 86 Prescot. The centenary was naturally celebrated in 1865 when Bro Gilbert Greenhall was Master. To celebrate the occasion the Provincial Grand Master presided at a special Provincial Grand Lodge in the Public Hall, Warrington when Bro Greenhall was invested as Provincial Senior Grand Warden. This morning occasion was followed by a service in the Parish Church and a Banquet, followed by an evening concert at which the members in full regalia entertained their ladies and friends. How things have changed! The Bi-Centenary was in 1965 when the Grand Master, the Earl of Scarborough, came and presented the Bi-Centenary Warrant.

The name of Gilbert Greenhall is now remembered in this hall by the lodge bearing his name (founded in 1869) and two chairs for deacons which bear that lodge's name in the anteroom to the large lodge room. This main temple is now re-decorated in more modern style and with a remarkable set of banners that have been created in the last two decades by Bro H. Boscow. These emblems of the lodges regularly meeting here recalls those days when the words now normally restricted to Provincial Grand Lodges—'Do you find them so ranged under their respective banners?'—could so well refer to the more homely surroundings of a lodge premise like this one. Certainly the array of banners here, mostly made by one hand, gives a sense of unity and congruity to this meeting place.

There are, too, other indications of the past in this room. The large tracing boards of the Lodge of Lights are on display and there is a charming kneeling stool with its raised armrest and two chairs that came with the True Light Lodge that previously met at Newton-Le-Willows but now meets here. There is also the unusual lectern for the chaplain's use. It is in the shape of an eagle, like many used in parish churches, and has of course a reference to St John the Evangelist, one of the patrons of masonry in its medieval and pre-Union days. This lectern also belonged to the Lodge of Lights.

Perhaps the most surprising feature in the room is a small coffin which is displayed 'with the emblems of mortality' during the ceremonies in this room. These items belong to the Lodge of St Austin's which was warranted as late as 1921 and numbered 4335. It took its name from the Austin Friary which existed in the town until the reign of Henry VIII. Its first IPM was, perhaps not surprisingly, WBro Sir Gilbert Greenhall Bt, CVO. Certainly the association of these third degree items with a lodge that had such pronounced ecclesiastical associations seems right and proper.

As you leave this hall housing the Warrington Group, now used by 22 Lodges and 5 Chapters, and stand in the street outside you can look to the left and see something of the Warrington in all its country town glory of days gone by. There are the ceremonial gates, the park and mansion that reflect a past which is now in danger of being swamped by the architecturally humdrum of a more quick-service age. One is glad to think that for the masons of Warrington somthing of the valued past is also behind them within the walls of their hall. There is indeed much there that will intrigue any mason.

One of the many fine jugs on display.

WHITBY

The Hall of the 'Golden Lion'

WHITBY IS NOT only famous for Captain Cook, the novelist Bram Stoker (creator of 'Dracula') and the unsung hero of the Battle of Trafalgar, Admiral Sir Robert Moorsom. For freemasons it is noteworthy as the possessor of a Masonic Hall with a distinguished-looking façade and a no less fascinating interior.

Turning left from one of the town's principal streets above the harbour you enter John Street, climbing up towards the summit of the town. On the left amongst three- and four-storeyed substantial terraced houses, you suddenly encounter the stone front of the hall with its arcade of three large arched windows on the ground floor, each window showing a very prominent keystone. Above these windows runs a frieze of square and round medallions, also in stone; the one on the left shows a square, maul and chisel, the one in the middle a pentalpha with a G at the centre and that on the right a square, plumbline and level.

Above these windows again there stand four round-headed lancet windows, the outer ones single and the two in the centre joined into one larger, stone-framed with a pierced stone circle above them. Still further up the façade there lies an open book in stone with a square and compasses extended upon it. All these items are crowned by a wide spreading gable roof with a sphere at its pinnacle and a descending decoration like stiff stone lace all the way down below the projecting eaves. It is a frontage with modest but notable dignity and though one now enters the hall by using a somewhat insignificant doorway to the right of the ground floor arcade you sense already that those who could outwardly so adorn their building must have other treasures that the visitor can appreciate.

The oldest lodge in Whitby was that of the Golden Lion in 1764, warranted in that year on 25 June as No 127 in the Antients Grand Lodge. It met first at the Golden Lion Inn, Golden Lion Bank, a hostelry which is still in existence and where one can see the original Lodge Door with the Tyler's hatch in it. Sadly the lodge was erased in the following decade due to a failure in making returns to the Grand Lodge.

The second lodge formed in Whitby belonged to the Moderns, was numbered 423 and warranted on 3 February, 1772. This lodge met at Buck Inn, St Ann's Staith, in 1771 and then at Mrs Mary Ellerby's Plough Inn in Church Street the next year. By 1785 it was registered in London as the 'Britannia'. Yet sadly this lodge was also erased in 1790 for making no returns though it in fact continued to minute meetings up to 13 February, 1792!

It was then that the present Lion Lodge, first numbered 561, was warranted on 14 January, 1797, and subsequently re-numbered until on 6 July, 1863 it became the 312 of today. This lodge started its life at the Golden Lion Inn like its earlier namesake, but after 16 years it moved to the Freemasons Tavern in Baxtergate. As we have the continuous minutes of the lodge from 30 January, 1797 we are able to follow the progress of the 'Lion' in its change of venue.

The minutes show, interestingly, that the first 15 members of the Lion Lodge were joining members from the Brittania, and as early as 18 December, 1797 there is no record of the presentation of the lodge jewels once belonging to Brittania for the use in the new Lion Lodge. By 1813 it is recorded that 'Brother Mathew Creaser, Mail Guard of Whitby and York, signified his intention to the brethren of this lodge that he intends to build a large and commodius (*sic*) room in his premises in Baxtergate suitable for a lodge room, provided the brethren of this lodge agree to remove there . . . ' The motion was put and unanimously agreed. On 21 June 'The Worshipful Master orders the Brethren to assemble here at 9 o'clock tomorrow morning in order that the procession may be in readiness to proceed to Church in due form at a quarter past 10 o'clock when a sermon will be preached on the occasion by Brother Andrew and from thence to the new Lodge room in Baxtergate. So as the whole of the brethren may be present at the time of its dedication'.

Matters were not left in too spiritual an atmosphere, however, for on 21 December 'Matthew Creaser, the Landlord of the present Lodge room signifies his intention to the Brethren of this Lodge that he expects to be paid a yearly rent of £20 for this room in future'. On the matter of whether or not the brethren 'disapproved of such an unreasonable demand' it was agreed that 'no rent whatever to be given and the Lodge be postponed until matters can be settled'. It was; for the minutes tell us that on 25 July, 1814, 'Matthew Creaser having left this situation, Brother Sawden has taken the house and placed in it people suitable to carry on the business of an Inn as before and has offered the Lodge room to the Brethren without any rent trusting to their generosity as Masons . . . '. That was not enough, however, as the masons were too aware of what happened but recently and so a bond was entered into between the lodge and Bro Sawden to the tune of £100.

It was as well they did this as in October (17th) Bro Sawden asked the lodge members at a meeting if they would continue with Mrs Wilson who was taking over from him and pay *her* a rent. The answer was a straight 'NO' but they would happily continue as they had agreed with Bro Sawden. It was then, when the said Mrs Wilson also moved a year later, that the Lion Lodge also left and for the next 44 years met at the Angel Inn, albeit still in Baxtergate. Problems of meeting and certainly providing space for other degrees now began to emerge and on 21 June, 1858 we note that it was 'Resolved to erect a Freemasons Hall'. In July they recorded that their tender of £75 for the land at West Cliff, and £725 for the erection of a building there, had been accepted. This area, incidentally, was developed by George Hudson the Railway King, with the Khyber Pass being cut out of the cliff in the 1840s and the gridiron pattern of the West Cliff area following. The location being fairly central and the chance of having a site which faced a main road in a new residential area must have pleased the lodge members and not least those newly prosperous Master Mariners who appear to have formed more than half the membership of this seaport lodge. Sadly George Hudson went

A view of the Lion Lodge room looking west.

312

bankrupt early in the new district's development and one can therefore only assume that since the Abstract of Title to the hall details all the parties concerned as creditors of George Hudson the sites were sold off at a rather cheaper rate in order to produce capital which would meet some of Hudson's debts.

The hall took about a year to complete, having the Stone Laying Ceremony on 8 September, 1858 with the subsequent Consecration on 16 August, 1859. The minutes record in 1866 that there were plans for the further alteration of the building but to date it has not been possible to discover what these were or indeed whether they were wholly or partially undertaken. What seems certain is that most of the existing premises are much as they have been for the past 130 years and certainly the visitor will sense the atmosphere of tradition and continuity that pervades the dining hall and temple.

The lodge purchased the adjoining house in about 1950 and incorporated the lower ground floor of this adjoining property with the dining hall to provide the entrance to which I have referred, the entrance passage being the present foyer and bar with a cloakroom. From this foyer there are two double doors opening into the dining room. The purchase of the adjoining property and the provision of another entrance permitted the removal of the central entrance in the arcade referred to and the demolition of two small rooms, one either side of the original central entrance, formerly a cloakroom and bar, and thereby enlarging the dining room to its present size.

You turn then from the end of the entrance passage by a door to the left to find yourself in the ground floor dining room. The room is no more pretentious than an ordinary masonic dining room needs to be and its main interest consists not in its furnishings so much as its wall features. These include a set of Hemming miniature tracing boards for the Craft degrees and an oil painting once presumably used as a ceiling adornment since it shows two interlaced triangles with a G at the centre (as on the front of the building) but surmounted on a blazing glory and with tongues of flame from each of the inner angles, and above it an All-Seeing Eye in the clouds casting rays of light on the symbol below. Before the days of painted ceilings or brass Gs suspended permanently in a Hall it must have adorned the inns with distinction.

There are also two striking portraits of local masonic personalities: one being of the late Earl of Zetland, who was both local Provincial Grand Master and then Grand Master of the United Grand Lodge, and presented to the lodge in January 1888. The other being that of a much earlier Master of the lodge, a true Master Mariner, and no less than that same Navy captain, Robert Moorsom, who was later to distinguish himself at Trafalgar, carry the great banner of Nelson at his funeral cortege from the Admiralty to the Cathedral of St Paul's, only to see it torn to ribbons and shared by his seamen over the grave, and thence to become at last a full Admiral of the Blue with a knighthood into the bargain. We learn that this active sailor lived with his father in Whitby and married in the year 1791 and joined the Lion Lodge in 1798. He was again on shore from 1801 to 1803 until war was declared and it may not therefore surprise us to see from the lodge minutes that he was Worshipful Master in 1802.

Yet the most unusual framed board in the corner of the room nearest to the Master's chair at dinner is one obviously connected with the Royal Arch, a painted floorcloth now consigned to a minor place but emphasizing all too clearly features of that Order which we shall do well to restore to prominence today. The picture is as follows.

At the top of nine shallow steps stand three minute red stools clearly intended for the Principals. Behind them, and towering over them, stands a white altar of incense, or pedestal of classic design, bearing on its top a gold coloured Ark of the Covenant. This Ark has on its side the Hebrew letters which read 'Kadosh Lo Adonai' (Holiness to the Lord) and standing, not kneeling, on the top of the Ark are two Cherubim with blue and red robes and wings aloft. Between them is a vertical golden circle with a golden triangle touching its sides within. Around the Cherubim is the heavy stone arch with the two uppermost stones removed and laid aside thus permitting a few rays of light to penetrate the Arch from above. The arch is supported by two classical columns that rest on the 7th of the nine steps mentioned already. Around the base of the central pedestal and giving the

Left: *The Royal Arch Principals' board.* Right: *Masonic symbols appear on the exterior of the hall.*

impression of a deep recess are representations of the chequered flooring that now adorns our Craft and RA meeting places. There is no date for this work but it has all the appearance of being early nineteenth century and may well be pre-Union. Its value in turning an Inn room from being a lodge into a Chapter would have been instantly recognisable.

We now take a winding stair to the first floor where a landing, two small preparation rooms and the main temple are situated. In one of the small rooms there are two further items of great interest. One is a ballot box of Victorian design and in the shape of a traditional Noah's Ark. Its presence here from an earlier age of masonry only serves to emphasise the maritime connections of this hall and also to remind freemasons that Noah was one of the first characters honoured as a builder and craftsman. The other item is a magnificent Tyler's sword of the 'wavy' variety which we have noted elsewhere in our Northern travels (see eg. the Hall at Alnwick) but the sword here is a specially fine one. It reminds the viewer that when first introduced in masonic ceremonies it was meant to convey both the ideas of the flaming sword which drove off Adam and Eve from the Paradise Garden and the serpent which had brought about their downfall from grace.

It is high time, however, to enter the Lion temple. We will be immediately reminded of this ancient lodge's name as we see a beautiful white representation of a lion couchant, sculptured from a Maltese stone, in front of the Senior Warden's pedestal. It was presented to the lodge in 1860, shortly after the lodge had begun to reside here, and it again reminds sailors of an older generation of yet one more of England's great naval connections.

The room that we have entered by one of two handsome wooden doors in the west, though one of these is false, is not overlarge but elegant, spacious and seemingly all of a piece. Most striking are the three timber pillars grained to simulate marble and about 12 feet in height, one each of the Ionic, Doric and Corinthian order, which stand at the north-east and north-west corners of the chequered floor carpet and just to the left of the Junior Warden's pedestal and on the carpet's edge. Above them and hanging from the centre of the gently bowed ceiling, with its panels representing the cloudy canopy and the stars in their constellations, is a most exquisite Victorian chandelier with candleholders that were manifestly made for gas brackets and have now been beautifully adapted to electric light. It can be seen why there was no place for the hanging G.

On the west wall, in two small and one large panel picked out in white and Craft blue, are the two oldest warrants of this building and in the centre a huge painting in original form of Faith, Hope and Charity. The female figures stand on a chequered flooring, each bearing the symbol of their Virtue—a cross, an anchor and with small children—whilst before them is a VSL with square and compasses and above them another All-Seeing Eye shedding rays of light on their heads.

The main furniture, the chairs and pedestals of the Master and two Wardens were presented to the lodge on 19 December, 1864 by different brethren and their unity of texture and design creates this overall effect of the hall having always had this sense of being created 'at once'. The chairs are distinctively mid-Victorian with Gothic window-style backs but each bearing at their centre the implement that indicates each distinctive office. The cream candlesticks and pillars on the Warden's pedestals blend with the larger pillars already noticed. One unexpected feature of the main officers' chairs is that when they are used for the Principals in the Royal Arch their heads swivel round to display their appropriate RA emblems. The chairs also have side arms which become a lion's paw and claws at their extremities, and these arms are reproduced on all the chairs in the east. Above the Master's chair the east end is made up of lovely leaded lights displaying many masonic emblems but these of course are concealed by a dark curtain during the times of meeting.

The deacons sit in specially designed Victorian seats bearing their emblems as customary today but the jewels that they wear are unusual. As a visitor will see they comprise the square level and plumbline and bear the motto *Ich Dien.* Very few lodges in England have such insignia and Lion Lodge is one of the few that remains. Two other officers sit in somewhat unusual places—the Secretary by the NE pillar, and the Treasurer at the SE corner. There are also three Volumes of the Sacred Law opened during each meeting—one on the Master's pedestal, one on the faldstool that stands below and in front of him and where the obligation is taken, and one on the SW's pedestal. It is worth remarking that the VSL on the faldstool is probably the original 'Book' of the lodge and is mostly marked at St John, chapter 1 which was again much used in the early days of the lodge. It is also worth remarking that the rough ashlar at the Junior Warden's pedestal is placed on a craftsman's sledge at its foot and not, as many expect, on the pedestal itself.

Yet one of the greatest and most remarkable features of this delightful meeting place is the series of wall plaques and large-size tracing boards that cover all the north and south walls of the Temple. They are about 10 feet high and 5 feet broad and they add a remarkable sense of history and achievment to this lodge room.

The tracing boards, apart from being authentic mid-Victorian designs, are not unlike those in many other places but the Mark and Chapter boards naming Past Masters and Principals would easily serve as excellent tracing boards in both these ceremonies. The former is of the Streonshalh Lodge of Mark Master Masons, No 337 and between the two lancet-style panels of names there is a scene, as if through a metal grille, showing all the main features of the Mark degree with a suspended keystone above a central wicket as the central figure. Done in the Mark colours it is a noble decoration, having been presented at the close of last century.

The latter panel is the name board of Brittania Chapter No 312 which celebrated its bi-centenary in 1983. This shows all the Chapter banners in due array with a broken arch as the central design. Besides these boards there are the name boards of the Lion's first century and another that will complete the second century in 1997.

Here there is a hall that can only be described as a 'hidden gem'. Little would many who pass it outside guess at the tranquility and dignity within. It is an oasis for the practice of masonry that has come unsullied from the past and I have not the slightest doubt that those who are responsible for it today will maintain its charm and its character. It is a memorable hall well worth a visit.

The 'Ceiling' Board.

WHITEHAVEN

An Antient Centre of the Cumberland Coast

ON AN ELEGANT, carved mahogany stand in the centre of the lodge room at College Street, Whitehaven hangs the well preserved and precious warrant that shows without question that the Sun, Square and Compasses Lodge, No 119, has been in regular existence from 18 May, 1768. It was a lodge formed under the 'Old Constitutions granted to his Royal Highness Prince Edwin at York, Anno Domini Nine hundred and twenty-six' and the warrant authorises 'Mr Jeremiah Elliott, one of our Master Masons, Richard Boardman, his senior Warden; and James Macdonald, his Junior Warden, to form and hold a lodge of Free and Accepted Masons aforesaid, at the sign of the Sun and Sexton, in the town of Whitehaven, and County of Cumberland'. The Warrant is signed 'Lan. Dermett, Grand

Whitehaven Masonic Hall looking west with illuminated globes and delicate organ casing.

Secretary' and registered as Vol 5, Letter E in the Grand Lodge archives of those days. The No. was then 157.

It is this Antient lodge whose hall we are next to visit, and a guide to Craft masonry in the present Province of Cumberland and Westmorland, published in 1879, some twenty years after the present hall was opened, states correctly that it is 'a Masonic temple that is excelled by few anywhere for capacity and completeness'. In terms of a meeting place for a moderately-sized seaside town such as Whitehaven, this is certainly the case and for the purposes of the lodges and chapters that currently meet there it is both adequate and worthy.

Yet it was almost a century before the freemasons of this port had their own

The Master's pedestal alcove with pediment detail (above) *showing rich detail work. Notice the globes by the pedestal whilst the globe adorning the pillar is illuminated.*

meeting place. The finding of some old minute books from the year 1804 enabled the members here to discover something of their pre-hall days but it is interesting to note that there there was no name of the first lodge until 1855 when certain brethren went to London and waited upon the Grand Secretary who asked them to choose a name and they chose the present one. The warrant, incidentally, is printed in ordinary letterpress and on a sheet of foolscap rather than on the more elaborate parchment on which documents were issued by the Grand Lodge subsequently.

The records open appropriately on the Feast of St John the Baptist and the officers having been appointed and 'taken upon them their respective offices, the whole body went in procession to St James's Chapel, where they heard an excellent sermon by the Revd. Mr. Armistead. Having returned in excellent order, the day was spent in harmony and love'. It is interesting to note that masons present that day came from Cork, Woolwich, Downpatrick, Ayr and Manchester. There were 72 members on the role of the lodge.

If their meeting place was still the same as at their founding they were soon to move, for in 18 months they are shown at four different places. When leaving the house of Mrs Sloan it is quaintly reported that 'while they regret the necessity of quitting her, they approve of her endeavours to please'. Her efforts were clearly not enough!

It is on St John the Evangelist's Day, 1804 that the title of Square and Compass is used, as found in the Treasurer's subscription book of 1805–6, though normally the title of the lodge was simply No 157 AYM (Antient York Masons). The removals still continued—in 1809 to the house of Ann McMellon, Blue Bell, Tangier St; in 1812 the house of John Slee, Three Tuns; and the same year to John Walker at the Blue Anchor and here the lodge was stated to 'be held at the Union of the Two Grand Lodges'. It is well to note what it was like at these various hostelry gatherings and in 1817 we note that at the Three Tuns they 'sat down to a plentiful dinner where love and harmony crowned the festival, with a sufficient quantity of enlivening fluid to drown dull care, and parted at the usual hour of ten o'clock perfectly satisfied with each other'.

By 1858, having further removed to the Packet Inn and thence to the Black Lion Hotel, King Street, the increased number of members caused another transfer to a more commodious room at the Globe 'until better arrangements could be made'. The following year the present building was bought for £608 and by a Trust Deed dated November 29, 1858. The property was conveyed to and vested in Bros Joseph Fletcher, James Dees, Henry Spencer and James Jackson. An amount of £453 was spent in altering the premises to meet their new needs and thus the final cost was over £1000. To meet this outlay a 'Masonic Hall Company' was formed and the members of the lodge became shareholders. In the next 70 years another £1000 had been spent on further improvements and in January 1902 the original Board or Trustees conveyed the premises to the Trustees appointed by the lodge itself.

Thus was established the more permanent home of this already long-standing lodge, and the centenary meeting was to take place where masonry has continued to be practiced for a further 120 years. It is a hall with its fair share of interesting contents.

The approach is discreet. Set in a quiet street in the centre of town the visitor mounts a flight of steps to enter the long corridor that leads from the front door. On the ground floor one finds the dining room with its unusual collection of life-size portraits of famous Past Masters of No 119. Thomas Magreevy was the leading light, being Master nine times in the period prior to his death in about 1825. We know of seven names of members, (Dodd, Cook, Quin, Rispin, Bateman, Harvey and Burney). There were possibly a few more, none could write and there were no minutes. There was also Major Fletcher who was WM for most of the years from 1850 to 1855 and ensured that the lodge which had failed to register on the books of Grand Lodge was again restored to its proper recognition, whilst another is Bro Patrick Quin, a mason for 51 years, who, with a fellow

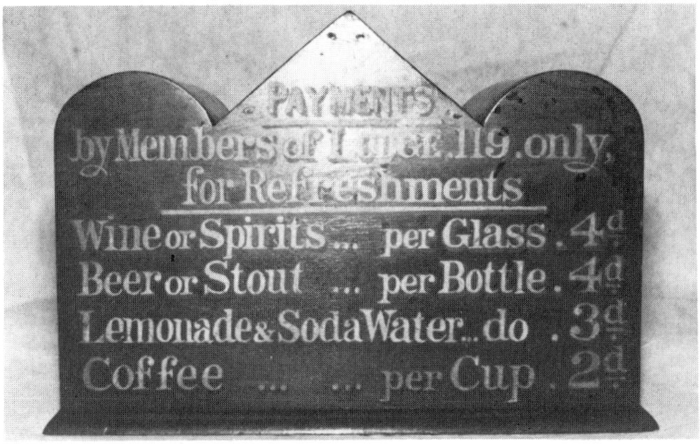

Above: *Refreshments in a previous age.* Right: *An original 'floorcloth'.* Below: *distinctive pediment above the Mark Masons PM board.* Left: *The Warrant of the Sun, Square and Compasses Lodge.*

coalminer and Bro Alexander Cook, gave so generously from their meagre means that when the lodge was at a low ebb they alone prevented it from falling into disuse. Major Joseph Fletcher and Henry Spencer also joined the lodge from the Midlands. They were men 'of substance', and their support financial and otherwise led to an immediate and lasting revival. Alexander Cook died in 1860, and Patrick Quin in 1874. Quin was locally considered the oldest mason who ever lived. John Thompson, one-time Provincial Grand Treasurer and brother of an Archbishop of York, is another that is portrayed and a latter portrait is of John Barr in his robes as First Principal of Sun, Square and Compasses Chapter. The warrant for the Chapter is also on proud display and dates from 1862. There is also a most distinctive Chapter carpet which not only conveys most effectively as sense of subterranean chamber but also displays a circle of the Signs of the Zodiac surrounding the pedestal that is set within it.

In the displays on the ground floor one also sees many items of special interest. The lodge still has sets of cutlery stamped with their own lodge number and a range of china (cups, saucers and plates) embossed with their own crest. There is an intriguing relic from earlier days—a wooden notice board that announces the payments due "By members of Lodge No 119 only, for Refreshments

Wine or Spirits	per Glass.	4d.
Beer or Stout	per Bottle.	4d.
Lemonade & Soda Water	do	3d.
Coffee	per Cup	2d.

The lodge also sported a pair of cut glass decanters in old green glass, bearing the sun, square and compasses emblems and marked 119 and 138, and these decanters are set on a silver trolley with a handle so that the beverages in their containers could be easily moved along the tables. There are mugs with much masonic symbolism obviously used for ale or beer and there are pink and white plates with their own pre-Union emblems. By the time one has walked around the dining room and the bar area one is already aware of the aura of tradition and character that still pervades this Antients temple.

Mounting to the next floor by means of the usual winding staircase we enter the original, if also partially modernised, lodge room. One's eye is immediately drawn to the delicate alcove in the east. It is set between two broad, half-projecting, straight white pillars with golden scrolled chapiters. In the alcove itself stands the WM's chair which dates from about 1820. It is of simple oak but with a covered red seat set within a semi-circle of four slender pillars, the former two of which carry a delicate golden arch having a black keystone at its peak, and the two rear pillars carrying a semi-circular frame on which rests a golden rising sun with projecting rays and a red star on its case. The whole effect is both modest and yet impressive.

Above this alcove and still between the white pillars there is a curved cornice with gold decorated motifs and at its centre a golden sun in glory, having a human face with a shining gold star on its forehead and a blue shield over its mouth bearing the number 119. This feature completes the whole effect and rightly enhances the place where the senior officer of the lodge has sat throughout the hall's history.

In front of the Master's chair is a pure white pedestal bearing a square in gold whilst flanking it are two very well-preserved globes of the terrestrial and celestial spheres held in oak brackets and on similar tripods. The effect is to draw the visitor's mind back to that pre-Union period when lectures on such subjects were part and parcel of the lodge's usual activities. Next to the Master's alcove, and also to the left of both the SW and JW's chairs, there stand a trio of lofty wooden pillars on the top of which are other globes, though these are made of glass and are illuminated during the ceremonies. They obviate the need for candles and also illustrate the older tradition of having only one pillar and light at the principal officers' chairs. They were the gift to the lodge in 1873 of Bro the Rt Hon G. A. Cavendish-Bentinck, MP, who affiliated in May that year. His reason for presenting them underlines the practice, even then, of emphasizing the importance of lectures, He said, 'On his last visit to the lodge, when he had the pleasure of hearing Bro Gibson explain the second Tracing Board, he regretted to observe that the columns representing the Ionic, Doric and Corinthian orders of architecture, were very improperly represented by those in the lodge. He had therefore conceived it to be his duty and privilege to provide others, which would correctly represent those Orders, and enable the lecturer to teach with accuracy and precision, and by them help the lofty and sacred truths which they symbolically represent'. They are certainly a most distinctive feature of this hall.

One cannot leave the east without referring to the delightfully embossed cover of the VSL on the Master's pedestal. Its age is shown by the number 138 (granted in 1832) and it bears not only four motifs of the square and compasses at the corners of the cover but a large radiating sun at the centre with an open book, named Holy Bible, and on it the square and compasses once again.

One of the many Masonic jugs kept at Whitehaven.

Looking to the west one sees the elegant cabinet for the warrant standing at the lodge centre, a tripod and its suspended smooth ashlar on the floor behind it, and then a large raised and wide stool for candidates. On the floor of the lodge for the MM degree is laid a very much used and decorated cloth bearing the emblems that are in most other lodges reproduced on a miniature trestle board at the Master's pedestal.

The Wardens' chairs have nothing of the character of the Master's but the SW's chair, like the Master's, is said to have once belonged to an older local lodge, that of Concord or Concordia, founded in 1805. When that lodge ceased in 1837–8 its equipment was on sale in the market place. The JW's chair of the set is last mentioned in the 1880s but then disappeared. To the right of the Senior Warden's place is a charming organ with a large mahogany surround inlaid with marquetry and displaying on side panels a number of masonic implements amongst natural plants. At the top of each of these panels is, on the left, a glorious sun face and, on the right, a crescent moon also with features. A sun, square and compasses in scroll work surmounts the whole organ case with its gold painted pipes.

Four other items in this lodge room remain to be described. Just inside the entrance on the left the visitor will be struck with a most delightful oak Honours Board for Mark Master Masons. The board is headed with a curved wooden arch having a keystone and the Mark circle of letters at its centre and below the arch, on a painted panel, the representation of Adoniram looking to the east from between the pillars at the Temple door. He is flanked by two Mark scenes—the work in the quarries and the carrying up of cedars from Joppa. The presence of this item very much underlines the link, throughout the life of this lodge, between the Craft and the other degrees, as was common in Antients lodges. Not only did the lodge work the RA degree as part of its Antients warrant—and hence the late appearance of a separate Chapter, but it is in this lodge that there is the only mention in Cumberland of the Cryptic degrees (October 14, 1804), which required also the working of the Mark degrees, but in 1805 the cash account of the lodge records 'an item of 2s 7½d, paid for sending a KT certificate to a brother in London. In 1809, Patrick McFadian was tried by a committee of Knights Templar, and was admitted.'

The lodge also had its own embossing stamps and these are used to this day. The typical decorated presses stand by the Secretary's table and visitors will be supplied not merely with the Craft boss but one for the Chapter also. The lodge also has some very fine early Victorian Lodge officers' jewels made in fine silver and bearing the sun motif above the appropriate emblem. The Tyler's sword is also very much more 'commanding' than most used by that member of the lodge. It would have done justice to a knight at arms and may even have descended from the time when a knightly ceremony was common in No 119.

Such is the meeting place of masons in this distant corner of our island kingdom. As they continue to treasure its past and its present one can only hope that many more will come to enjoy its memories and its treasures in the future.

YORK

The Hall at Duncombe Place

THERE MUST BE MANY visitors to York who, on approaching the west end of the Minster from the station, fail to cast a glance sideways and see, on their right, a quiet little corner of this ancient city. He would notice a stretch of lawn, some rose bushes, a tall but single pine, a beech tree, a paved footpath making a right angle between two buildings, one of stone and one of brick, and a discreet but handsome stone doorway in the angle of the two. If the visitor was a freemason and he did manage to see the modest courtyard he would perhaps be pleasantly surprised for along the top of the tall-windowed stone building to the right he would read some tell-tale words—*Audi, Vidi, Tace*. In terms of the city and council in which he found himself they may best be translated—Eer all, See all and Say nowt.

This tiny, quiet and pleasant enclave just off one of the city's main tourist routes is Duncombe Place. It houses the Provincial office of Yorkshire, North and East Ridings, but it was intended originally as the home of one of the oldest lodges in the city of York, Lodge No 236. Its setting, within a stone's throw and under the shadow of the Minster's great West Towers, only serves to emphasise the natural link that we have seen in several places in the north between church and Craft, between religion and ritual. It is devoutly to be hoped that there will never come a time when these two bodies will refuse to recognise each other.

It is worth noting that the constitution and warrant of Union Lodge (as it was first named) were presented on the seventh day of the seventh month of the year 1777. The members are mentioned in the warrant as meeting at Lockwood's Coffee House and even though the owner of those premises was initiated and made Tyler his occasional embarrassing absences from the outside of the door was one of the reasons given for the proposal in January 1786 that they should move and especially if there would be more accommodation and some space for a preparation room. Despite threats from the Tyler that he would resign, and prevent the regalia being taken away if they left, the lodge did move to the Theatre Coffee House in Top Lane. During the next three years there the first purchase of the books that now form the extensive library in Duncombe Place were made. Thereafter the lodge soon moved to the Golden Lion Inn situated in Thursday Market and settled down for 31 years.

During the 42 years that followed that tenure the lodge moved some 7 times and two of these were to Blake Street which once stood on the same ground as that now occupied by the present hall. By 1859 a special Committee reported that they had '(subject to the approval of the lodge) agreed with the proprietors' of the building in which the Provincial Masonic Lodge was housed 'for the purchase of the premises together with the front house in Little Blake Street for the sum of £550, the purchase to be completed on the 1st July'. As the money seemed forthcoming it was further resolved that 'in the opinion of this Lodge, the establishment of a Library and refreshment room is very desirable, and that the premises should be devoted exclusively to Masonic purposes and that it was not desirable that the present Tavern system should be extended'.

After a year spent in adapting the building for their use the lodge took up residence in what was now called Duncombe Place. It was not the only change. In 1861 the Corporation Street Improvement Committee decided that the narrowness of the throughfare was a serious hazard as great congestion was often caused. Discussion with the authorities took place and whilst the brethren were quite prepared for demolition of their building they were naturally anxious to obtain the proper compensation. In the end, writes the lodge historian, 'the lodge received £175 10 0d in cash and 293 square yards of land—which was a little more than had been asked'.

Building plans were commissioned and Bro Oates, a member of the lodge and an architect, submitted his suggestions. A London brother, J. Barton Wilson, made the drawings for the interior of the temple and the brethren were so pleased with the result that they gave him a vote of thanks and his draughtsman a gratuity of 2 guineas! On 8 September, 1862 the foundation stone and usual jar with 'relics' were placed at the north east corner of what was to be the lodge room, and on 2 June, 1863 an extraordinary lodge was called for the purpose of opening and consecrating this new hall.

Duncombe Place, York.

Yet the hall was not quite yet what we shall discover it to be when we enter it and behold its treasures shortly. The minutes of meetings held here from 1863 reveal that whenever there was a larger gathering—and the lodge was a premier one of the province with a growing popularity—the brethren always retired to some other building for the banquet. This evident deficiency and some others led to yet another committee being formed as soon as 1866, which reported a year later that 'the front elevation should be taken down and rebuilt 12 feet forward from the present foundation' thus giving a much larger dining area upstairs. The elevation was to be increased by 3 feet thus providing more space for a Steward's room whilst the removal of the winding staircase and the placing of the toilets in the basement meant a much larger foyer, better preparing room and easier access above.

The work was done 'at cost' for a final figure of £450 and whilst the hall lost its previous Doric porch (still outlined by the fresher stone projecting from the library wall) it gained the no less distinguished entrance of today. There will be those who would have liked to keep a true 2nd degree winding staircase (for a little glimpse of which the reader might care to see the hall at Barnstaple—Vol one in this series, on the South of England) but there is so much of truly antique interest still in Duncombe Place that perhaps the visitor can forgive the developers. Certainly anyone who attends the lodge and stays for supper in the upper dining room, with its U-shaped dining table and the views from the windows looking out on the

The three ancient tracing boards.

floodlit Minster, cannot but delight to have so ample a dining room made possible by these changes.

Nobody, in fact, casting that sideways glance to which I referred earlier, could guess at the tasteful corridors with their prints or the library just to the right of the main door with its lines of antique mahogany bookcases and the valuable works which they contain or the extending mahogany table made circa 1823 by Bro Raper of Davygate. Here, too, he cannot miss the two antique Wardens' chairs made of fruit wood which date from around 1770 but which were only presented to the lodge in 1930.

Much less would the casual passer-by, be he mason or no, guess at what awaits the visitor here as he leaves the library, descends three steps, turns a corner and approaches the shielded door of the classical-style temple that awaits him. You pass into the room by turning left or right around what is revealed as the organ casing and console that occupy most of the west wall. What then meets you are the 'Two pillars at the Porch or Entrance' representing B. and J. They are of wood and bronzed, 6 ft high and surmounted by Chapiters of pomegranates and above them the celestial and terrestrial globes. The golden network that covers the globes was presented by a Bro Jancowski who had created a bond between the York 'Union' Lodge and the 'York Lodge of Friendship' in Berlin, by his fraternal visit to the latter and their reciprocal visit in 1854.

It is facing out, between these magnificent pillars, that we see the organ in all its glory. It was described in 1865 as 'with ornamental front, gilded and decorated'. It was made by Denman of York and it was almost entirely bought by special subscription from the members, over and above their generous gifts to the fabric alteration expenses. In 1879 the organ was enlarged by a new and complete swell mechanism and reed stops.

Due to the fantastic cost of organ restoration, the keyboard was removed and an electric organ presented by WBro H. B. Raylor was fitted, the pipes and casing being retained.

It is now time to turn and begin to take in the majestic room that lies to the east. It is as if one were indeed being taken back into that very old freemasonry of which York has always proudly claimed to be the source. The dimensions (40 feet long and 30 feet wide), the sheer diversity of content, and the overall combination of the parts into what is an apparently harmonious whole make one pause and appreciate afresh the memorable nature of so much that English Freemasonry possesses.

Looking eastwards one makes out two larger-than-life figures standing in niches at the north- and south-east corners. They represent, of course, St John the Baptist and St John the Evangelist, the great parallels of pre-Union freemasonry, and they were gifts to the lodge from the Zetland Chapter in 1866. The figures are beautifully sculpted in Caen stone.

Taking next a first glance at the walls one notices that they are divided into panelled compartments by lofty pilasters crowned with Corinthian capitals, each compartment also surmounted by fully ornamented friezes and arched mouldings which merge into a curved cornice. The ceiling itself is divided into three sections—two of them admitting light through stained glass, whilst the third has panels carrying masonic symbols and the 12 Signs of the Zodiac.

Yet the most unusual feature that one sees here is 4 tassels hanging from the ceiling. (The interested reader will see a similar feature, though on a smaller scale, in the hall at Faversham, Kent. Vol. one.). These tassels were placed there by WBro Alfred Proctor at the turn of this century when he was Treasurer of the lodge, and are meant to represent the four cardinal virtues—Truth, Temperance, Fortitude and Justice. It is likely that Bro Proctor had read in old masonic lectures that these tassels should be placed at the four corners of the 'lodge' when the lodge was a platform board that was carried about, and on painted tracing boards at a later date they are shown in just that position. Their appearance here is a quaint but timely reminder of a feature of older masonry that could so easily be lost sight of—another link with the past for the YORK lodge, for that had become its name from 1870.

Running along the centre of the temple from west to east is a parallel set of five columns of classical style, made of wood and dating from the start of this hall where they are described as 'with globular shades for Gas light'. The columns themselves are carved to represent the 5 noble orders of architecture—Tuscan, Ionic, Doric, Corinthian and Composite—and each of the globes bears some masonic indication of the various degrees and orders that are practiced in this hall.

On the floor of the lodge there stands an item that was for many years the unique possession of York lodge until members of a visiting lodge were so impressed with the item that they introduced a perfect copy into their own furnishings. It is described in the lodge inventory of 1856 as 'Shears, legs, windless and cords. I pair brass blocks and cords. Lewis, Perfect Ashlar and Rough Ashlar and platform'. It was clearly meant at that time to be the replacement for the very first purchase of the old UNION Lodge in 1777 which is recorded on 4 August as—'Our Worshipful Master brought two brass blocks and pulleys which was approved of and ordered to be purchased . . . '. These happily were left intact when one of the few unreliable Treasurers in masonry, Bro Tomes, vanished to London 'having robbed the lodge of their assets' and taking money loaned to him by nine of the brethren. (For those wishing to compare similar sized and authentic features in a lodge the ones in Taunton and Weymouth are worth examining).

The delightful and distinctive mahogany Gothic type chairs for the three principal offices are adorned with masonic devices and seen in numerous places elsewhere but it is worth noting that these chairs were bought by their first occupants and then presented to the lodge as gifts after their occupancy of them. Their gifts have been most carefully preserved and handed on.

The pedestals for them and the Secretary were ordered rather earlier (in 1848) and the lodge granted the money for this as well as for the purchase of a floor-cloth. It seems however that the Treasurer was so intent on having a pedestal for himself that FIVE were in fact bought for £4 12s 6d each. Considering that the gilding on them with their distinctive painting then cost more than the mere joinery it is not surprising that this amount is not revealed. What you will see today is that the two pedestals of Secretary and Treasurer have been joined together and used as one ample writing desk for the Secretary alone.

The three candlesticks that now stand on the Master and Wardens' pedestals are also very fine, being again mahogany with silver sockets. How or when they came into the possession of the York Lodge is not definitely known but the inventories say clearly that they were once the property of the defunct Grand Lodge of All England. It is believed that they were probably presented by Bro Blanchard, proprietor of the York Chronicle, who was also Grand Secretary and the last surviving member of that body. In 1817 he handed to Lodge 236 many of its records and they are of course kept here in the library.

The chair that usually attracts the most attention in this hall is the one used by the Director of Ceremonies. It is an armchair adorned with the beehive and seven bees, and the plumbline carved on the back. It was clearly a Junior Warden's chair that at once symbolises refreshment and labour, honey and the busy bee. It was presented to the lodge by the executors of Anthony Buckle, principal of the Yorkshire School for the Blind, and Master of the lodge in 1879.

The other chairs that once adorned the temple—24 armchairs in 'Crimson Utrecht Velvet' made by Mr Duncan, cabinet maker of Minster Gates, are now happily in use in the dining room, whilst a further ten chairs, specially donated for the use of Past Masters, have stood on the dais here since 7 November, 1864.

With so much of fascination already described it might seem that there can be little left to look at. Such is not the case. There are at least three more areas needing our attention.

Left: *One of the old pillars with globe and netting.* Centre: *Grand Lodge of All England banner.* Right: *The Master's pedestal.* Bottom: *the library.*

The first is the 'Obligating Pedestal' which stands before the Master's chair, but on the floor of the lodge below the stepped dais. This also was once the property of the Grand Lodge of All England. In 1770, we read, on the feast of St John the Evangelist, Sir Thomas Gascoigne was installed Grand Master. He presented 'a most elegant cushion covered with Crimson Velvet and fringed with gold' for the Constitutional Rolls, the Bible, Square and Compasses. He also provided a mahogany pedestal of the Ionic order to support the three great lights on their cushion. That is the very pedestal seen here and though its original crimson cover is carefully preserved elsewhere (though used until 1930) we have yet one more link with a famous past.

The same is no less true of the Grand Lodge of All England board which dates back to 1778 and which was painted by Thomas Beckwith, a respected local artist and Masonic jeweller. It was given by a Bro Blanchard to Bro W. C. Turner who then presented it to the lodge in 1842. The board shows in the top half the vaulted crypt of a great church and then, below a decoration of oak leaves and mistletoe, the two great pillars, two pyramids with sun and crescent moon, the compasses and rule, with the plumbline, level and square at the centre. It is a design still familiar today in the bookplate of Duncombe Place library.

There are also three enormous boards on the north wall of this temple, measuring 7 feet high by 3½ feet wide, and filling the spaces there between the pilasters. They were purchased in 1851 and painted by Thomas Newnum, a lodge member. Their special distinction is that here, at last, we have direct evidence of how early lodges chose special passages for opening up the VSL for each degree. In this case the passages inscribed at the head of each board are:

1° *Psalm* 133
2° *Amos* ch.7, v.7
3° *Ecclesiastes* ch.12 vv.1–8

What will certainly surprise many masons is that they remain open to view throughout each and every meeting of the lodge. There are no curtains to cover those not needed as is the case elsewhere with wall boards.

Finally, in this magnificent and historic chamber, one cannot avoid the banners. There is the York Lodge banner with its four special devices, under which the brethren would sit when they took it to their Provincial meeting; the banner of the Grand Lodge of All England with symbols not too dissimilar to those of the 'Antients'; the banner of the Provincial Grand Lodge in 1821; and five processional banners which were those carried in public demonstrations by the masons. The presence of these superbly executed and well-preserved flags make this room just that much more a treasure house of the past for the present.

When anyone gathers in this hall with all its memorable connections and evocative furnishings there can only be a sense of great pride and pleasure that so much remains to us from days gone by. Perhaps some words from the distinctive closing hymn of York Lodge can best sum up this place that well deserves a visit:

Though frail our craft, our faith is bright,
That in our labours Thou art near;
From humble efforts thou wilt rear
A fabric perfect in thy sight.

HALIFAX

The Hall of the 'Other' Building Society

MASONIC HALLS VARY in their outward appearance considerably. There are those like the ones in Sunderland, Barton-upon-Humber and Alnwick which could not be distinguished at all, whilst others have simply a blue door or pillared porch and a modest masonic symbol to mark them out. The façades at Whitby and Berwick are much more obvious but it is not until the masonic visitor stands in front of the main hall in the town of Halifax that it is realised what a unique and striking declaration of the Craft there can be. One masonic writer has remarked that 'It reminds me of a veteran Provincial Brother well endowed with jewels'. That is certainly true though he also goes on to add: 'Bro Fielding in 1851 said that all secret societies agreed that it would be undesirable to meet at a public house. What would he have thought of the Hall? Bro J. W. Hobbs has said that a building like ours proclaims the fact that it is not the haunt of a secret society—"it is properly a Society having secrets"'. (*The Lodge of Probity No 61*, T. W. Hanson, p311).

On first encountering it in 1987 I could not myself avoid the reflection that it was singular to find this masonic hall facing the vast bulk of the Halifax Building Society structure across St John's Place. Even more of a coincidence was it that two 'building societies' should be in such juxta-position; and yet the Society that was set up to serve the 'popular and uninstructed world' was well-nigh anonymous as to its purpose, with its huge concrete walls, acres of glass and apparently shapeless, almost surrealist, form, whilst the home of the masons was evident and openly displayed, appearing like a cross between a set of respectable Victorian offices and a porticoed home. Certainly no-one could be in any doubt as to who meets here.

From what is now the landscaped walk-way of St John's Place with its arrangement of flowers and shrubs in stone bays, its pseudo-Victorian globe lamps and a solitary tree, one looks up at two storeys of tall sash windows, each with their rounded or shallow arched tops and each with a keystone in the centre of them. To the left of the impressive covered entrance way, and completing the first floor façade, is the gabled end of the temple. It is this feature that most catches the eye. It was designed, as was the whole frontage, by the same Bro Oates whom we met in the reconstruction of the hall at Duncombe Place, York. (See p132). The layout of the symbols on this frontage is as follows:

Between four pilasters with rich Corinthian capitals are six features. On the left and at the bottom is an altar with an open VSL on the top of it and on the front face the No 61 with PROBITY and a crossed square and compasses beneath. At the top and in the entablature are 4 triple taus around two interlaced triangles (the

Seal of Solomon) with a triangle at the centre, with 'Regularity' and 'Sincerity' on the interlaced triangles.

In the centre panel and on the three symbolic steps there rises a plain archway and within it the coat of arms of the United Grand Lodge of England with its cherubic supporters and an All-Seeing Eye shedding rays of light downwards onto the upraised wings of the angels. Above, also in an entablature, is some delicate scroll and foliage work with the date of the hall's erection (AL 5868) in a circular wreath at the heart.

The right hand panel has another altar similar to the first at the bottom save that in addition to another VSL it bears the inscription '448' with 'ST JAMES' below. Above this is another entablature with 5 Lorraine crosses, four at the corners and the centre one imposed on a Maltese cross, with the name 'Salamanca' on the belted surround.

The whole of this frontage is surmounted by a heavy triangular pediment marked with rows of projecting 'ashlars' and at the very centre of the triangular space a square frame containing a large keystone with a cramp, 53 and 53 to its sides and, below, the name of the local Mark Lodge, Fearnley No 58. The whole display is a remarkable exposé, at least to those in the know, of what transpires within. It is by far the most overt and unashamed declaration to passers-by that this is a masonic hall that I know and for this reason alone the hall is a memorable one. A Victorian but undated print of the building, however, shows no decoration on the facia.

The Lodge of Probity mentioned on this façade was founded in 1738 whilst its partner of St James was created just a century later. Both lodges, like so many others of which we have heard, had moved from location to location in an attempt to establish themselves satisfactorily though Probity was at the Old Cock Hotel for 95 years. As late as 1865, when the Provincial Grand Lodge of West Yorkshire was held in the Town Hall, Halifax, Lord Londesborough presented a roe and a hamper of game to Probity Lodge as they were responsible for the entertainments. These included a banquet at the White Swan Hotel, with a Grand Masonic Ball in the Assembly Rooms in the evening. Taking the banquet to that hotel did not at all please the landlady of their current 'home' at the Old Cock and as soon as she learnt of their intentions, and still a month before the Provincial gathering, Miss Young refused the use of their room for further meetings.

The seriousness of this kind of decision was all the more evident to a lodge that had begun to acquire a substantial amount of furniture. New tracing boards had been acquired the year previously, whilst in 1856 we read of Geo Jackson being paid 3s 6d 'for renewal of Floor Cloth in 3d degree'. It can be seen that the lodge was very refined in its equipment for working. In addition a new minute book for 1864 tells us of items that we can see to this day in the present premises. '2 Columns SD and JD' which are then referred to a year later as '2 Jupiters'. These were the Deacons' wands, surmounted with figures of Mercury, which are still used today. Previously the Mercury was a jewel for those officers but was then transferred to the top of the wands. There was also mention of '9 velvet gilt and blue rosettes' but by the time the lodge had moved to this hall there were only 6 left and they were now 'silver gilt and blue rosettes'.

Accordingly the lodge determined that whilst they must buy time they also needed to start looking for a more permanent home. A deputation waited on Miss

The west view with organ loft.

The coffered ceiling with constellations.

Young who agreed to a new rent of 10 guineas, but the search was on and though some offices at the old Calder and Hebble Navigation Co. building were not considered right the committee which had been set up now reported:

'Although the subject is not alluded to in the resolution appointing this committee, their attention has been drawn to the question of erecting a New Building for the accommodation of the lodge . . . the question is referred to the favourable consideration of every member . . . '. The result was decisive. They should build a new hall.

In July 1867 St James's Lodge had reached the same conclusion and were in earnest about making plans for a building of their own. Within ten days the Probity brethren had decided to act in conjunction with their fellow masons. Four days after that, on 30 July, the St. James' members paid the deposit for a plot of land in St John's Place, and by 20 August they had also agreed to join hands in the venture with Probity. The first joint Committee met on 27 August. This procedure alone shows both the common sense and determination that both parties shared in achieving their goal as soon as possible. Bros Jackson, Oates and Horsfall, all professional men, had an invitation to draw plans and by November 1867 their efforts were inspected by the brethren at the Old Cock Hotel. Considering the effect that these plans would have on the hotel's owner and her lettings this private review in lodge would appear to be rather 'cocking a snook' at Miss Young. One combined set of plans was to emerge from this gathering.

It was remarkable at the time, and is no less fitting to comment on now, that whilst the site for the new hall was named long before it was chosen for building it could hardly have been more appropriately named for St John's Masons. St John's Lane, leading to the south of the Place, was the old road once on the extremity of the town and was much more ancient than Prescott or Horton Streets. The lane led into Blackledge and hence the Parish Church of St. John the Baptist.

The corner stone of this new hall was laid by Sir Henry Edwards, Bart, MP, a PM of No 61, on 30 June, 1868. It was carried out during Halifax Fair Week and as it proved to be a beautiful midsummer day a large crowd of onlookers witnessed the ceremony, together with the procession of clothed masons from the Town Hall. By November 1869 the whole structure was complete and this time the Provincial Grand Master, the Earl de Grey and Ripon, performed the requisite ceremonies. One forbears to reproduce the fare enjoyed at the banquet on this occasion but it is worth noting that the tickets mentioned the venue as 'The Masonic Temple, Halifax' which is not the title now used.

It is time, however, to mount the steps and enter this building that was dedicated that day. The impression then, with all the furnishings and decoration in pristine condition, must have been especially pleasing for we can still gain a sense of the elegance and quality that must have been enjoyed as the brethren of these two established lodges at last entered upon an inheritance that was going to be more permanent and private than anything that they had enjoyed before. Here was no hostelry to be shared with the public, no room that hung on the whim of the landlord, no storage that might be invaded or tampered with, no temple that was makeshift and approximate. Here was home for the whole of the foreseeable future and they would be careful to ensure that it was maintained as such. It is no way meant to derogate from the special purpose for which this hall was constructed and has been maintained to say that one's main impression in entering it is to think of it as a good quality club.

That sense was enhanced for me when I learnt that from the beginning the two sharing lodges decided on the use of special rooms for their separate preparations and non-ritual meetings. It may be unusual, but it is here very relevant, to read a notice in the lofty hallway—'Applications for the use of the rooms of the Lodge of Probity and of St James' Lodge must first be made to the Master of the Lodge concerned, and the use of such rooms for Practices and Meetings shall then be arranged with the Manager of the Hall'.

To suit the deed to the word you turn off the main hallway into one of these rooms—that of Probity No 1061. It has a truly formal air with well-upholstered round back chairs designated for the WM, SW and JW, a solid table and fine carpet, pictures that are peculiar to the lodge's members and its past, and a fine display case full of masonic jewels. The whole maintenance of this room is the care and concern of the lodge which it serves and though the hall is a shared one there is this corner of it which proclaims for all time the special identity and private interests of one of the partners. I find the idea strangely moving and worthwhile. To see the ample Jacobean settle, the locally tooled Bible, the attractive decoration on the back of the door, and the countless mementoes of many members gave one a strange sense of sharing in a special way with this well-established and respected lodge. What is so memorable is the fact that for 120 years it has been a practice well maintained and never thought worth changing. It gave one a deep sense of stability and worth.

Passing into the hallway again one is struck by the reference to one of local masonry's great characters—Wilkinson Pool, Tyler for 31 years (1771–1802) who, we are quaintly told, 'was changed to the Lodge above' on 8 August, 1802, at the age of 71. It is to the area where he and his like would more happily reign that we now turn as we mount the gracious staircase with its wrought iron balustrade and the halfway landing under a striking bit of stained glass. This refers to the local name of the town, having the face of Christ with red hair and beard and a halo, on a chequered shield of orange and blue squares with the words 'Halez' and 'Fax' framing the head. It refers to the lodge, Halez Fax, No 4135. The stained glass windows in the building were made by a local glass merchant, R. T. Titley. The present proprietor, as well as his father before him, is still an active Halifax Mason.

It soon becomes clear that we have mounted three sections of 5, 7 and 15 treads in that order. We reach a stately landing with two lofty pillars and may notice that from one end of the space there leads off a room known as the St James's room, the private meeting room of the other of the building's founder lodges, and to the other side of the lobby is a room known as the REMBRANDT ROOM, which is the usual changing room used by others than those of the two main lodges. The Halifax Rembrandt Club was founded 10 November, 1875 and soon changed its name to the Halifax Art Society. During the eighties of the last century annual exhibitions of the members' works were held in this room and the name has survived even if the Club is long forgotten.

The main temple that leads off this landing is another masterpiece of solid Victorian construction. The semi-pillared walls, the lofty painted ceiling with its massive moulded corners and turquoise coloured cornice is just one more surprise for the visitor who might have imagined that this was but a modest gentlemen's club. Here, in the very heart of the building and quietly tucked away from any of a busy city's hubbub is a place of impressive elegance from a century or so ago. The furniture was built to match the surroundings and though not as decorative as its earlier comparisons elsewhere in these volumes it fully fitted its place and purposes here . . .

Yet here comes another surprise! Since I went to see this hall for the first time that prosperous Building Society opposite has failed to renew the lease and has demanded the use of this site for the extension of its own activities. There is therefore no point in my writing more about the glories of a hall that is no longer on view to the eager masonic caller. Happily the fine façade and the general interior of the building is to be preserved for posterity and one can only express delight that some of the Halifax's masonic past will be enshrined in the locality for others to see. The fate of this hall may perhaps be a fitting reminder to readers of what can all too easily happen to any property that does not wholly belong to local masons and if that is not adequately appreciated by those who have the privilege of using them. I can only fervently trust that all the other fine buildings mentioned in the three volumes of this series will be spared the loss that Halifax is now undergoing. We have here a heritage that we must surely do all in our power to preserve and protect.

The remarkable façade and portico no longer introduces a masonic hall.

61
PROBITY
448
S.JAMES

INDEX

People and Places

Object and Symbols

The Halls covered in other volumes in this series are:

The SOUTH

Barnstaple
Bath
Bradford-on-Avon
Brighton
Bristol
Canterbury
Cheltenham
Exeter
Faversham
Jersey
Langport
Lewes
Liskeard
Newport (IoW)
Poole
St Austell
Taunton
Torbay
Weymouth
Windsor

The MIDLANDS

Birmingham
Boston
Colchester
Ipswich
King's Lynn
Knutsford
Leicester
Letchworth
Ludlow
Norwich
Nottingham
Peterborough
Shrewsbury
Spilsby
Stamford
Stony Stratford
Warwick
Worksop
Great Yarmouth